Strategies for
SENIOR HOUSING UNDERWRITING

Evaluating Senior Housing Developments

Mortgage Bankers Association Of America

PROBUS PUBLISHING COMPANY
Chicago, Illinois

© 1990, The Mortgage Bankers Association of America

This publication is designed to provide accurate and authoritative information in regard to the subject matter covered. It is sold with the understanding that the publisher is not engaged in rendering legal, accounting or other professional service.

Library of Congress Cataloging in Publication Data Available

ISBN 1-55738-094-5

Printed in the United States of America

1 2 3 4 5 6 7 8 9 0

Table of Contents

About the Contributors

Arthur J. Corrazzini is an economic consultant based in Washington. Mr. Corrazzini undertakes economic and policy analysis under contract to government agencies, trade associations, and private firms. He has completed myriad statistical reviews and strategic planning studies, authored articles and publications, spoken before Congressional and Senatorial subcommittees, and provided technical and program planning assistance to various organizations. Mr. Corrazzini has served as Deputy Director at the Office of the Chief Economist, the United States General Accounting Office, Senior Economist at the Executive Office of the President, and was Chairman of the Department of Economics at Tufts University.

William J. Gabler is Vice President of Norwest Investment Services, Inc. in Minneapolis, Minnesota, an investment banking subsidiary of a regional financial institution. He has financed or developed over 5,000 units of housing for the elderly in his career.

Peter A. Gerard, Executive Vice President and Chief Financial Officer and principal of Westbrooke Hospitality Corporation, is a specialist in real estate and hotel finance with 16 years of experience in diverse industries and an extensive background in the hospitality industry. Mr. Gerard was an investment banker with both national and regional investment banking firms for more than 10 years. Prior to joining Westbrooke he was associated with the Dallas-based regional brokerage firm of Schneider, Bernet & Hickman as Senior Vice President, Corporate Finance. He has authored several published articles on and participated in the financing of hotels and other properties. Mr. Gerard holds a bachelor's degree from Yale University and an MBA from Harvard where he was a George F. Baker Scholar.

Gerry D. Glaser is Senior Production Officer of ABG Financial Services, Inc., in Minneapolis, Minnesota. ABG specializes in financing arrangements for multi-family housing, including congregate and assisted living facilities. Until recently, Mr. Glaser served as Vice President and Development Manager of Oxford Development Enterprises in Greenbelt, Maryland where he was responsible for the development of senior living facilities and nursing homes in the Mid-Atlantic and Northeastern United States. He first became involved in elderly housing in the mid-1970s while with the Ebenezer Society, a multi-level geriatric campus in Minneapolis. Ebenezer owns and manages several hundred units of housing and nursing home buildings including the nation's first cooperatively-owned congregate facility in suburban Minneapolis.

Richard R. Jaffe is Chairman and President of Retirement Housing International, a Dallas consulting firm providing feasibility studies, pre-project planning, and marketing strategies for developers and operators of retirement housing properties, and specializing in the turnaround and workout of troubled or underperforming retirement housing properties. Mr. Jaffe has successfully completed 14 turnaround projects and has performed over 60 feasibility studies and strategic marketing plans for client projects. He is a founder of the National Association for Senior Living Industries (NASLI), and has served on their Board of Directors since its inception.

Terry W. McKinley is the Regional Vice President of the Minneapolis-based ABG Financial Services, Inc., a mortgage banker and coinsuring lender. ABG specializes in arranging financing for multifamily housing, including various forms of congregate and assisted living facilities. Since entering the multifamily industry in 1969, Mr. McKinley has held senior finance and development positions with such firms as Merrill Lynch Huntoon Paige in New York, Norwest Bancorporation, Minneapolis, and the National Housing Partnership in Washington.

Leon A. Pastalan, Ph.D. received his Ph.D. from Syracuse University and is currently a Professor of Architecture, College of Architecture and Urban Planning at The University of Michigan. He is also director of the National Center on Housing and Living Arrangements for Older Americans. Professor Pastalan is a researcher of long standing in the field of environments for the elderly, with an emphasis in several areas, including sensory deficits, spatial behavior, and housing. He is the author and editor of many books and national publications resulting from his work, including most recently, *Environmental Context of Aging: Lifestyles, Environmental Quality and Living Arrangements*, Garland Press, 1979; *Man Environment Reference 2*, The

University of Michigan Press, 1983; and *Retirement Communities: An American Original* with M. Hunt, A. Feldt, R. Marans, and K. Vakalo, Haworth Press, 1984; *Lifestyles and Housing of Older Adults: The Florida Experience* with M. Cowart, Haworth Press, 1989.

Alan F. Scott is President of Zaremba Development Company and Zaremba Construction Company, and has been involved in the development of 60 multifamily developments. As President of Zaremba, Mr. Scott has constructed over 3,000 apartment units, 1,200 in the South Florida market alone. Operations in which he has been involved include multifamily condominiums, nursing homes, congregate housing, and single family developments. In 1986, Mr. Scott served as Chairman of the National Association of Home Builders Special Committee on Senior Housing, and is Treasurer and Board Member of the Cleveland Building Industry Association and serves as the Apartment and Condominium Council Chairman of the Ohio Home Builders Association.

Morton Yulish joined Laventhol & Horwath as a Senior Principal in 1987, with the merger of Public Demographics, Inc. (PDI) with L&H. Mr. Yulish supervised the development of ElderCare MARKiTS, L&H's unique market feasibility analysis for senior living facilities and ElderCare Site Profile (ESP), a proprietary senior market data product. In the six years since he and two associates founded PDI, Mr. Yulish has served as principal-in-charge of numerous specialized market analyses and program assistance, as well as demographic and economic analyses, for numerous public and private sector clients in the real estate development community. He served the United States Department of Housing and Urban Development (HUD), Yonkers, New York, the Westchester County Executive, and Hartford, Connecticut. In 1979 Mr. Yulish was a private consultant to HUD, the U.S. Conference of Mayors, and the Economic

Development Administration on economic, housing, and other community development subjects. He also served several corporate clients, consulting on such matters as market research and demographic analysis. He has lectured extensively on housing and commercial development topics for such organizations as the National League of Cities, United States Conference of Mayors, and the American Economic Development Council. Susan B. Brecht and Howard K. Peters, who are located in L & H's Philadelphia office, assisted Mr. Yulish in writing the article.

Introduction

Historically, the elderly have been housed according to how the society perceives its older people. Among the hunting and gathering societies where surpluses were unknown, when an individual could no longer support himself, he was considered a burden. As culture and technology progressed and societies became more sedentary and productive, the elderly were considered the source of wisdom and knowledge. The concept of the extended family became fundamental to the fabric of most cultures, and multigenerational housing patterns emerged.

In the nineteenth century and with Western industrialization, society began to feel more responsibility for the elderly. Unfortunately, this often meant finding a place to store what was considered an obsolete segment of the population.

At the beginning of the twentieth century, the U.S. population over 65 numbered only 3,084,000, or approximately four percent of the total population. Advances in medical technology had not yet affected population growth or life span as they would over the next 89 years. The U.S. was still very much a

1

nation of immigrants, and people's living patterns more closely reflected those of their motherland than those of their new home. Ethnic neighborhoods flourished. Within this segment of the population, multi-generational households prevailed—the housing needs of the elderly were provided by the primary family grouping.

The wealthy segment of the population addressed the housing needs of the elderly differently. Having the financial resources to do so, the wealthy elderly tended to maintain residences independent of younger generations. This meant either maintaining independent households or living in resort hotels, probably the first real examples of independent and assisted living facilities for the elderly. Recognizing economic opportunity, these hotels catered to the needs of elderly by providing them with an appealing, comfortable environment, including medical facilities. The great resort hotels of the early 1900s, such as the Biltmore in Palm Beach and the Bedford Springs in Pennsylvania, are two of the earliest examples of the "upper-end" independent living facilities that are now the trend.

Improvements in communications and transportation led to a breakdown in many traditional patterns, including housing patterns. After World War I, mobility became the norm rather than the exception, both in economic status and location. For the first time, a significant percentage of the population spoke of the place where they grew up as "where they used to live." This new mobility had a significant impact on traditional housing patterns, particularly the traditional multi-generational living patterns of ethnic communities. Young men and their families tended to follow job opportunities and not return to the family home. As a result, an increasing number of elderly found themselves without a family homestead in which to grow old.

Medical advances resulted in a decrease in infant mortality rates and an increase in life expectancy. Combined with the significant growth in birth rates before World War I and after

World War II, the result was obvious—a dramatic rise in the number of persons in the 65-and-over group. By 1990, the number of persons over 65 in the U.S. will exceed 31,000,000 or 12.7 percent of the population. In fact, according to Pannell Kerr Forester's health care consulting group, 5000 Americans turn 65 each day.

The significance of these growth numbers is amplified by the fact that this segment of the population's life expectancy continues to increase. As a group, those over 65 are healthier and more active than ever before. Individuals within this group will require housing for longer periods, and their demands for services will be greater than in the past.

These trends have not gone unnoticed. Over the last few decades federal and state government agencies have spent untold hours and dollars to analyze and develop programs to address the challenge of housing the elderly. While much of the effort has been directed at the provision of adequate housing for the poor, a number of programs, most notably loan guarantee and tax incentive programs, have provided the private sector with significant incentives to enter the senior housing field.

Despite these programs and the general public's increasing awareness of the growing challenges and opportunities in this area, much of what has been done has failed from either a services or financial viability standpoint. According to Al Holbrook, manager of health care consulting for Pannell Kerr Forster, in 1989 there were approximately $1.5 billion worth of retirement community projects in the U.S. that could not meet their financial obligations.

A major contributor to this problem has been the lack of comprehension of the scope and breadth of services required by this growing population, including the needs of the healthier new entrants, and the implications of "aging in place." Developer ignorance of the management-intensive nature of the facilities has resulted in many failures. Still, many developers, spurred by tax incentives and low cost loans, continue to enter the senior housing market.

The demographics of the elderly population reflect considerable opportunity for the resourceful retirement community developer or investor—the numbers themselves spell out the growing need for such housing. Even with this ever-increasing market, competition for tenants is fierce. Players in the senior housing industry must arm themselves with knowledge to survive and prosper. The wisdom of experience related in this book should prove helpful to the hopeful.

1

Meeting the Housing Needs of the Elderly

by Arthur J. Corrazzini

America is in the midst of a demographic revolution which will influence every facet of our society. The following is a discussion of the demographics of the elderly in the U.S. in terms of number, income, and resources. I will identify trends as well as current and future living arrangements, needs, and preferences of the elderly.

By 2030 there will be 64.5 million elderly people in America, constituting 21.2 percent of the population, almost double the current figure of 11.8 percent. The population 65 years of age and over will comprise a larger portion of society, and the average age of the elderly will increase as more people live into their late 70s, mid-80s, and beyond. Over the next 20 years the population aged 65 to 74 will increase by only two percent, while the 75 and over group will grow by fully 48 percent. The population aged 85 and over will almost double (see Table 1).

The housing industry has shown enthusiastic anticipation of this broadening market for new forms of elderly housing. Whether such expectations are accurate predictions of future activity or not, it is clear that we are entering a new demographic era, and that the "graying of America" introduces new opportunities and challenges. As a society, we have just begun to evaluate the consequences of this demographic shift. The unique and profound ways that longevity will influence the housing and housing finance sectors make it important that we consider the present and plan for the future.

Current Elderly Living Patterns

Demographic data suggest that to the extent longevity alone creates new shelter needs for the next 20 years, those needs will focus on individuals in the 75 and over age group. In contrast, the number of people in the 65 to 74 year age bracket is not expected to increase until after 2005. As important, up to now this age group has not demonstrated a strong desire for an altered lifestyle or new forms of retirement housing. Instead, a change of circumstance (usually poor health or the death of a spouse) is the most common cause of a move to retirement housing. Hence, few 65 year-old couples move to retirement communities and the average age of entry is 77.

About 70 percent of elderly people live in single-family homes, 65 percent own their homes, and 19 percent rent hous-

Table 1. Population Projections

	Millions of Persons			% Increase 1987-2005	% Increase 2005-2020
	1987	2005	2020		
65–74	17.4	17.7	29.9	2%	68%
75–84	9.6	12.8	14.5	33%	13%
85+	2.9	5.7	7.1	95%	24%
Total	29.9	36.2	51.5	21%	42%

Source: U.S. Census

ing. Only one in ten lives in either a retirement community or a senior citizen building.

Some 66 percent of elderly people "age in place"—they are happy with their housing situation and have lived in their current communities for over 20 years, and half have lived in their current residence for that period. A full 61 percent are worried about having to move from their present home. In a recent American Association of Retired Persons (AARP) survey of 1,500 elderly persons, 85 percent of those surveyed disagreed with the statement, "What I'd really like to do is move from here."[1] The same survey found that women over the age of 80 were the group most unwilling to move.

Those most willing to move were individuals with college degrees, those with household incomes over $32,000, men and women under 70 who live alone, and people in declining health.

Those elderly who are easiest to serve with new forms of housing, the 65 to 75 age group, do not constitute a growing segment of the elderly population and exhibit a general reluctance to move. Other groups within the elderly population whose numbers are growing rapidly and who we might think of as benefiting from a move to a retirement community, such as isolated elderly in remote locations without easy access to support services, health care facilities, or a socially supportive environment, may also be reluctant to move. This group may also be financially unable to relocate.

A closer look at patterns of living and income levels underscores these points. About 8.8 million non-institutionalized elderly people live alone, a 76 percent increase in 16 years (see Table 2).

Presently, about one-fourth of the 65 to 74 age bracket, one-third of those aged 75-84, and one-half of those aged 85

---

[1]Understanding Senior Housing: An American Association of Retired Persons Survey of Consumer Preferences, Concerns and Needs. 1987.

Table 2. Number of People Living Alone

(in millions)

	1986	2005	2020
65–74	4.381	4.960	8.370
Male	.928	.943	1.591
Female	3.453	4.017	6.779
74–85	3.490	4.990	5.660
Male	.640	.899	1.019
Female	2.850	4.091	4.641
85+	.950	2.680	3.340
Male	.189	.536	.668
Female	.761	2.144	2.672
Total Living Alone	8.8	12.0	17.1

Source: Tabulated from tables appearing in *The Prevention and Elimination of Poverty Among the Elderly Living Alone.* ICF Corp. for the Commonwealth Fund. 1987.

and over, live alone. Eighty percent of these are female. The probability of living alone increases with age. Unless living patterns change by the year 2005, more than 40 percent of those 75 and above (7.6 million) will be living alone. Eighty percent will be females who, despite physical impairments, will resist a move to more supportive environments.

Today's Elderly— Affluent or Disadvantaged?

Several reports have emphasized the growing affluence of the elderly. Much of the analysis has focused on the decline of overall poverty rates among the elderly, or on average income figures. Adequate attention has not always been paid to variations in income levels by living status.

Recent analysis undertaken for the Commonwealth Fund provides a better picture of the income status of the elderly. In 1986, the average income for all elderly was $23,906, a figure that compares favorably with the overall population. However, the income of those living alone was only $14,090, while that of those living with others was $31,797. Only four percent of all elderly married couples were living in poverty, while nineteen percent of those living alone were poor (see Table 3).

Projections indicate that over the next 20 to 40 years the real income of the elderly will rise due to an increase in pension benefits, social security, and IRA benefits. While the percentage of those living in poverty should also decrease, high poverty levels are likely to persist for those elderly living alone.

Table 3. Income of Elderly

	1986	2001–2005	2016–2020
All 65+	$23,906	$24,906	$31,072
Living Alone	14,090	16,383	17,900
Men	16,000	—	—
Women	13,600	—	—
Living with Others	31,787	32,140	41,536
% Below Poverty Line			
Married	4% (<$6,802)	—	—
Living Alone	19% (<$5,393)	19%	15%

Source: Same as Table 2.

Policy Alternatives

Demographics and income statistics, in combination with survey results indicating a general desire to "age in place," suggest two broad courses of action:

- **The adoption of policies to encourage the creation of shelter and service complexes, responsive to the health and social support needs of its aging residents.** Such policies would, through demonstration and consumer education, entice the elderly to change residence, move, and lessen their attachment to familiar surroundings. Alternatives for all income groups would be offered. The focus of the effort would be on those elderly aged 75 and over. Only gradually, if at all, would the newly retired move in large numbers to these new housing complexes. However, in the long run the sheer magnitude of the population shift may introduce entirely new living patterns that are difficult to forecast.

- **Acknowledgement of the preference of the elderly to "age in place"** would demand the creation of programs to assist the elderly in making their existing residence more suitable to their needs. The challenge will be to identify an appropriate policy mix, and then implement its components.

Retirement Housing Industry

Population projections have generated interest in the elderly as a social group with enormous future housing requirements. Although the younger (65 to 74) and more mobile elderly population is not growing and most elderly resist moving, many institutions have become suppliers of elderly housing.

In contrast to the single-family housing marketplace, both not-for-profit and for-profit entities are anxious to build and operate facilities. Potential suppliers of housing services include:

- residential builders/developers;

- commercial developers;

- the hotel industry;

- church organizations;

- senior citizen organizations;

- hospitals and related health care operators, and

- nursing home operators.

Motivational factors such as concern for the needs of the elderly, profit potential in some projects, and economic efficiencies in spreading hospital or nursing home overhead costs have resulted in a rapid expansion of the number of facilities in some markets, with differing results on the "broad but thin" senior housing market.

Careful project planning is extremely important. New projects may experience fill periods of 18 to 24 months, adding considerable risk to project financing. Slow fill periods are often attributed to such factors as oversupply, poor project planning, and a general reluctance by the elderly to move into the type of project under construction.

Although there is intense industry interest in the construction of new retirement facilities, the information necessary to measure the overall rate and direction of expansion is scarce. A national inventory was undertaken in 1981 that identified 2,364 retirement communities.[2] Some of those communities were mobile home parks (15 percent), others hi-rises (23 percent). Approximately one-third had nursing home capacity and 38 percent carried a religious affiliation. A rough estimate of the number of dwelling units derived from these data indicate a figure of 720,000.

Most project planning must be performed at the community level—local field surveys can identify existing capacity, vacancy levels, and rental rates. While plans may be formulated without the aid of current figures, a more recent national inventory of retirement communities would be helpful to both the building industry and federal and state governments in their formulation of long-term plans and policies for elderly housing.

Those actively involved in developing new retirement facilities separate the market into three submarkets, differentiated by age and physical characteristics. The AARP defines these groups as:

- "go-go"—healthy and highly mobile;

- "go-slow"—marginally healthy and mobile;

- "no-go"—in declining health and mobility.

We must consider the variation in income levels within each of these groups. Housing has been marketed to specific, perceived current needs of each group: adult communities for the highly mobile, and nursing homes for those in declining health.

If there is a problem with this approach, it lies in the specialized nature of the products offered. For example, a healthy,

---

[2]A Directory of Retirement Communities in the United States, National Policy Center in Housing and Living Arrangements for Older Americans, University of Michigan.

mobile 65 year-old couple may choose to move to an adult community setting and, within a relatively short time, be faced with health problems or the death of a spouse, necessitating a second move. A 70 year-old living alone may move to an apartment setting, only to find that, in a few years, some personal health care services are needed daily, and are unavailable.

Unless each type of facility is widely available, people unable to live with complete independence may be forced into an inappropriate facility. (A common example is an individual who needs minimal health care being placed in a nursing home.)

Both not-for-profit and for-profit entities recognize that the challenge is to find ways to create integrated retirement complexes, able to respond to changing health and social needs of a population which may pass through stages of health and mobility.

A role for government must also be defined if there is serious intent to make such facilities available to all income segments of the population. Two principal approaches to senior housing facilities dominate the marketplace:

- **congregate housing,** a specially designed apartment complex that provides shelter, meals, housekeeping, transportation, and social activities;

- **life care communities,** elaborately designed complexes structured to address the problems of both shelter and health care. In this type of facility, meals, housekeeping, and medical care are available for a fee.

Both housing concepts attract the aged. In the AARP survey of elderly, about half of respondents expressed interest in congregate and continuing care facilities. The life care community concept has come under scrutiny due to the elaborate and expensive nature of the undertaking.

Life care communities are characterized by three major components: residential living units, an activity center, and health care center. The health care center usually contains both infirmary, intermediate care, and nursing home facilities.

Costs generally consist of both a sizeable entry fee (about $70,000), and a monthly payment—affordable only to middle to upper income segments. Centers are owned and operated by religious organizations and other not-for-profits, and are often financed by tax-exempt bonds.

Problems have developed in the operation of many life care communities, including deficiencies in health care coverage, financially insolvent developments, deprivation of new cash infusions due to occupant longevity, and increases in medical costs. Some 10 percent of all projects have failed financially. (Despite a tenuous financial status and emerging fraud problems, the potential attractiveness of the life care concept should not be overlooked.)

Because of the lack of comprehensive, systematic data on which segments of the elderly population enter retirement facilities, it is difficult to state which groups are underserved. There exists a perception that congregate facilities are expensive to build and difficult to finance. Private, profitable undertakings appear to be targeted to the upper-income market, while many not-for-profit groups find it difficult to obtain financing to build at all.

Federal financing and insurance programs are open to not-for-profit entities, but often the initial project planning funds and required equity and debt service reserves limit participation. These same requirements also add appreciably to the financial risks associated with for-profit ventures, and tend to drive those ventures toward the creation of retirement alternatives that can only be afforded by upper-income segments of the population.

Middle-income retirees have the fewest options. For low-income retirees, not-for-profit involvement (via federal direct loan programs) has been extensive, but this is changing.

"Aging in Place"

Recent analytical work on the living patterns of the elderly revealed the preference of the elderly to "age in place" or retain residency in their homes. Research also shows that a significant portion of older Americans have a "dwelling-use problem"—functional impairment due to a physical disability or health problem that indicates the need for home modifications or support services. In many instances, the individuals will neither move to a more appropriate setting nor physically alter their current surroundings. Whether their reasons are due to income constraints, personal preferences, or an actual lack of alternatives, is unknown.

A recent AARP survey of the elderly attempted to identify what older people would have done had they anticipated having to adjust to the changing circumstances associated with longevity. The results indicate that a relatively small but significant portion of the home owning population would consider such options as a second mortgage, modification of their home to include a second apartment, or entrance into a reverse annuity mortgage agreement. About half of those surveyed would consider a move to a life care or congregate housing facility.

Because housing is the largest single asset of the elderly and the total amount of home equity held by those aged 65 or over is estimated to be $600-800 billion, economists and policy analysts are eager to facilitate the conversion of those assets into spendable income. Even those elderly living alone and those living in poverty often have some equity value in their homes (see Table 4). Among the poor, however, 45 percent have $10,000 or less in equity.

Therefore, housing is considered a vehicle to alleviate the income problem. The following are several proposals set forth to use these assets:

- **line of credit**—not repayable until death, and, presumably, the sale of the asset;

- **sale or leaseback**—wherein the home is sold to an investor and rented back to the present homeowner;

- **reverse annuity mortgage**—the homeowner takes a mortgage on his home and uses the proceeds to purchase an annuity. The difference between the mortgage payments and annuity payouts is net income to the recipient;

- **term reverse mortgage**—a payout is made to the homeowner drawing down on his equity, allowing him to incur rising debt; the loan is then becomes due and payable at a specific future date.

Methods exist to structure such mortgage instruments so that repayment is deferred as long as the individual resides in the home. However, despite the popularity of the concept among academics and segments of the policy community, both the elderly and the banking sector are reluctant to support the idea.

Deferral of repayment and continual disbursement of funds for what could be a lengthy interval generates considerable default risk for banks. The longer the maturity of the loan, the greater the default risk. As the size of the loan balance rises, the value of the property against which it is made becomes more uncertain.

Some experts assert that to become attractive to the financial community, such loans need to incorporate decreasing in-

Table 4. Home Equity Holdings of the Elderly

	% With Home Equity	Average Amount
All Elderly		
Poor	54.27	$20,502
Near Poor	59.61	26,415
Non Poor	79.86	40,143
Living Alone		
Poor	51.11	19,500
Near Poor	54.07	24,946
Non Poor	68.41	34,757
Living with Others		
Poor	62.64	22,491
Near Poor	71.31	28,769
Non Poor	86.00	$42,440

Source: Same as Table 2.

terest rates, be pooled by a lender and then sold into the secondary market, and be insured.

Programs have begun in ten states. The difficulty of the concept and the complexity of the transaction limits the number of completed transactions to about 1,000 annually. State involvement may refine the transaction, but broad acceptability on the part of lenders and borrowers appears distant.

Nonetheless, efforts to change the lending community's view of the elderly do highlight for the lender long-term issues that should be examined. The financial industry has failed to acknowledge demographic facts—many more elderly people will want to borrow for household needs, much in the way growing families borrow—to cope with changing living requirements. The challenge to the financial community is to creatively meet these needs.

2

Approaches to Elderly Housing

by Terry McKinley, Gerry Glaser, and William Gabler

In less than eight years—not coincidentally the period since the demise of major federal housing subsidy programs—America's multifamily housing production industry has discovered a new focus for its creative energies. As demographers have documented the growth of the market for elderly housing, developers and health care providers have proceeded with a panoply of "products" designed to serve it.

New housing concepts such as CCRCs (Continuing Care Retirement Communities), ILFs (Independent Living Facilities), ACLFs (Assisted Care Living Facilities), PCFs (Personal Care Facilities), and ReSCs (Residential Service Centers) have

21

evolved as developers have searched for the most profitable combination of shelter and services for particular groups of seniors. Lenders have watched this evolution from a distance, waiting for the most secure lending opportunity to be discovered.

The following is a discussion of housing alternatives and lending possibilities which are, in some cases, time-tested, and in others, designed to meet the evolving, sophisticated set of needs and demands of a diverse group of home buyers and renters. Included is an economic and demographic background for the current senior housing situation, popular housing choices of the elderly, demographic trends affecting the retirement industry, the economics of health care, and opportunities for the developer.

Until the mid 1970s, the multifamily housing industry viewed the elderly market as consisting of two basic groups: the sick and the poor. The needs of these groups were met primarily by not-for-profit and proprietary nursing home operators, and not-for-profit and profit-motivated developers of subsidized housing. The remaining elderly population was thought to reside in their own single-family homes, or in the homes of relatives.

To the typical multifamily developer, the market consisted of those needing either nursing care, or the benefits of federal subsidy programs (Section 236 or Section 8). No real options existed for the marginally healthy, so effective management for nursing home operators often involved maximizing the availability of various federal medical subsidy programs (such as Medicaid), rather than operating an appealing, competitive facility.

Financing options were also limited, consisting of conventional mortgage loans (from a few life insurance companies interested in nursing homes), full recourse tax-exempt bonds for health care providers, and federal insurance/subsidy programs (such as Section 232 for nursing homes, and Sections 202, 236, and 8 for low to moderate income housing). For the lender, underwriting consisted largely of studying the sufficiency of the applicable subsidy program to meet operating expenses and debt service, with some attention given to management's credentials.

In the mid to late 1970s, some developers shifted their focus to a new segment of the elderly population: individuals who *choose* to live in surroundings amenable to their physical limitations—where services such as housekeeping and meals could be purchased. Both large and small developers devoted considerable resources to this new market for two principal reasons:

- **Economics:** As people age, they tend to accumulate financial assets. Federal housing subsidy programs have been replaced as a financial resource by equity in the homes of the elderly (estimated to be in the billions of dollars). A popular belief is that most older individuals look to home equity to invest in retirement housing rather than a world cruise.

- **Population:** In addition to growth in the numbers of seniors through advances in medicine, older seniors are living longer. In 1950, those aged 65 and over made up just 7.7 percent of the population. They now constitute 12 percent of the population, and are projected to grow to 17.3 by the year 2020. (Source: U.S. Bureau of Census, "Demographic and Socioeconomic Aspects of Aging in the United States.") The fastest growing segment, those aged 85 or more, has increased from 0.4 percent of the total population in 1950 to 1.25 percent today (2.7 million) and will increase to 2.75 percent (7.1 million) by 2020. As a recent *Time Magazine* article of February 22, 1988 stated, "By 1995, the population of the average United States town will look like Florida's population today."

These factors, combined with the realization by increasing numbers of the elderly that their lives can be enhanced by moving out of single family homes, result in an explosion of opportunities for the apartment or nursing home developer.

Options

The American Association of Retired Persons (AARP) has assembled a comprehensive list of the types of housing available to elderly persons in a publication titled "Housing Options for Older Americans." According to the AARP, popular choices of the elderly are:

- **Single-Family Homes.** Many elderly Americans live in their own single-family homes. Typically, they have no debt outstanding on the house, an expression of their financial and physical independence. However, as the occupant becomes less physically able to care for the house it becomes more expensive to maintain.

- **Apartments.** Increasingly, elderly Americans are turning to apartment living. The federal government has assisted in the construction of hundreds of thousands of subsidized rental units, and elderly persons occupy many conventional apartments. Rental apartments are an attractive option for many of those aged 65 and over who have taken advantage of the capital gains exclusion on the sale of their home. These persons stay financially liquid by investing the proceeds of the home sale and renting an apartment.

- **Mobile Homes.** The South and Southwest United States contain many mobile home parks occupied both by "Snow Birds" (Northern residents that spend their winters in the South) and year-round residents. In the northern portion of the United States and in rural areas, mobile homes may be purchased for less than a new single family home.

- **Condominiums.** Condominiums offer the tax and financial advantages of home ownership without the maintenance burdens of a single family home. Condominiums seem to be particularly attractive to those in the age brackets of 55 to 70. In some instances, apartment buildings are converted to condominiums and the existing residents are able to purchase their units at an attractive price.

- **Cooperatives.** In a cooperative, the person owns a share of the corporation that owns the building, and has a right to lease a unit (versus a condominium, in which a person owns their own unit and a share in the common areas). They have the same advantages over single-family homes as condominiums.

- **Retirement Communities.** Retirement communities are planned to offer the elderly a variety of housing options, such as single-family homes and apartments. They often have on-site health care facilities and offer a service package that can be tailored to meet resident needs.

- **Home Equity Conversions.** Many elderly people who own their homes are equity rich and income poor. Reverse mortgages, life estates, and other options allow the elderly to take advantage of the equity in a home while they are still living in it. In a reverse mortgage, the lender makes a monthly payment to the homeowner, adding the additional amount to the mortgage on the property. In a life estate, an outside party buys the home from the elderly person but allows them to live there during their lifetime.

- **Accessory Apartments.** These are variations on the "in-law apartment" in which an apartment is created in the home for an older person, often a relative.

- **Echo Housing.** Echo houses are smaller, detached units located on the same lot as an existing house. They foster more independence than an accessory apartment because they are detached from the house. The resident has a greater feeling of freedom and may come and go easily while maintaining privacy.

- **Home Matching.** In home matching, an elderly home owner shares their house with another person who can provide service, companionship, or simply rent in exchange for a more affordable housing unit. These situations can allow an older person to live in their home for a longer period of time if the new occupant is able to provide maintenance for the unit.

- **Share Housing.** Share housing brings together a group of elderly persons in a residential setting. Many shared homes are rehabilitated for elderly persons, and some have suites where persons have their own bedrooms and share common living spaces.

Clearly, options for housing the elderly are varied and changing. For demographic and economic reasons, the successful multifamily developer will focus on a narrower band of housing options for the elderly, concentrating on either semi-independent/congregate housing, or assisted living/personal care.

According to the U.S. Bureau of Census, the growth rate of the population aged 65 years or older will slow in the early 1990s and remain relatively constant through the balance of the decade, unlike the strong, steady growth of the last 20 years. This demographic plateau, a result of the childbirth nadir during the depression era through World War II, will show fewer individuals the 65 years of age or more in the 1990s. The greatest effect will likely be on single-family builders who have developed a strong niche in "empty nester" or pre-retirement housing. Business may be less brisk and more competitive.

Ironically, while the growth of the population segment 65 or more years of age slows and plateaus, the growth of the population aged 80 or more years will skyrocket. Evidence of this trend is apparent: all one has to do is view Willard Scott's daily salute to centenarians on "The Today Show" to realize that living 100 or more years is a growing reality, and possibly a birthright of American life.

It is clear that the span of life has increased from "three score and ten" to an even "four score and counting." While today's "four scorers" will likely be healthier than their recent kin, they will still experience the difficulties that come with age. Consequently, market size and demand will grow in this population segment, as their housing decisions become less discretionary and more driven by need.

Marketing may become more difficult for the developer who stubbornly holds to "independent housing" in a marketplace of elderly citizens that will be less independent, looking toward the shelter/service feature of specialized housing to maintain their quality of life. Developers with the foresight to deliver an attractive mix of shelter/services to this growing client base stand to make a good profit in the 1990s.

While demographics will drive the market, the economics of health care will also have an influence. People 80 years of age and over have the potential to break the health care bank if service continues "business as usual." This segment's health care spending pattern is an estimated five to six times that of the rest of the population. More stringent Medicare hospital cost containment practices have emptied hospitals of their "cost plus" elderly patients and filled nursing homes with residents who are older and sicker than the facilities are prepared to serve.

A *Time Magazine* article dated February 22, 1988 stated that if patterns of health care consumption remain unchanged, there will be sufficient demand for a new 220 bed nursing home to be opened every day between now and the year 2000. Concurrently, it appears clear that the political clout of senior citizens will make long-term care insurance a birthright for all. Attempts to husband resources and ration care (risk management by federal and private insurers), will restrict service to those who truly need high cost, institutional long-term care. Those not requiring such care will require new alternatives.

Opportunities

These factors present a challenge for the multifamily developer: rapid growth of a "need driven" 80-and-over market that will require a richer mix of services and health care than most multifamily developers have offered before. For the forward-thinking developer, opportunities are tremendous. Consider:

- **Existing Properties.** Many perfectly good properties are languishing in Southwestern states and other soft markets, products of the "gold rush" of facility development in the 1980s. Many of these projects were simply a decade ahead of the market. Demand for many of these properties by the 80-and-over segment should emerge in the 1990s. Opportunities exist for developers with strong marketing and management skills who could acquire these moribund properties and reposition them to serve this need-driven market.

- **New Properties.** The retirement "gold rush" of the 1980s was aimed primarily at the top 15 to 20 percent of the income bracket—"Cadillac communities." This segment's membership is small, fickle, and financially independent, with many options. The middle class market has generally rejected luxury retirement living, but their attitudes change when longevity makes the single family home less convenient, functional, or appealing. There is a vast, untapped market for "Chevrolet" and "Buick" retirement housing projects, offering a few more programs and services to satisfy the 80-and-over market.

- **Subsidized Projects.** The political clout of the 80-and-over group should result in new and renewed forms of subsidized housing for the elderly. Regardless of administrations, there is likely to be some form of federal subsidy (direct or indirect) or financial participation. It is more likely that federal subsidy vehicles will require the financing resources of states, sponsorship of not-for-profit institutions, the taxing and land resources of local municipalities, and the organizational skills and entrepreneurial talents of the private development sector. Targets of such aid will be those people over 80 whose needs are not great enough to qualify for rationed healthcare/housing programs, but whose resources are inadequate for purely private sector housing/service options.

- **Assisted Living.** For the intrepid multifamily developer, the greatest opportunities are likely to be found in the development and operation of assisted living communities. Operated on a smaller scale of 30 to 60 units, these free standing projects will offer an abundant mix of services to benefit the need driven population aged 85+. The developer's niche will be an attractive residential environment, well placed and in existing neighborhoods, offering the ambience of a distinctive residence while providing a full menu of support services to sustain residents until entry to a nursing home is necessary. As the retirement community industry emerges, governmental oversight will be stringent, despite the minimal commitment of federal dollars toward assisted living services. The assisted living marketplace will be considered a regulatory "gray zone" in which housing and health care combine to form private sector options for long-term care.

Conclusion

Senior housing is enduring the inevitable shake-ups, shake-downs, and shake-outs that are by-products of a youthful industry's exuberance and inexperience. Hard lessons are being learned quickly and an array of products are being developed to serve the market niches that comprise the 65-and-over marketplace.

The factors of strong demographic and economic fundamentals are the senior housing market-makers of the 1990s. While the dearth of depression-era babies will slow the overall 65-and-over growth rate, the promise of a longer life will eventually swell the ranks of those who are "four score and counting."

Providing housing and services to this older, need driven market segment represents the greatest potential to developers. However, serving these older segments will require greater market sensitivity in forming the shelter/service equation, and meticulous marketing and management to achieve the early, timely occupancy required for success.

3

Housing Design for the Elderly

Leon A. Pastalan, Ph.D.

Introduction

A new phenomenon has appeared in our society, the phenomenon of mass longevity. Mass longevity is so new that our society has not had time to evolve appropriate institutional responses to deal effectively with its many manifestations. For example, there does not exist at this time a value consensus regarding a model of successful old age. "What do you want to be when you grow old?" has not been a question seriously dealt with on either a personal or collective basis. The recent emergence of so many elderly people has caught our society unprepared. We are unprepared to respond informally in terms of commonly held values about what the expectations and conditions of old age should be and unprepared to respond formally in the sense that there are very few national policies and programs that address themselves to the special needs of the elderly.

The purpose of this chapter is to provide an overview of present knowledge regarding who the elderly are, why they have special housing needs and what types of housing design are indicated by these characteristics and needs. Hopefully, this overview will promote active support for good housing design and neighborhood planning for the elderly and will encourage all relevant publics to take strong and active roles in the initiation, planning and operation of programs to prolong independent living arrangements and improve the quality of life for older people.

The elderly perhaps better represent a cross-section of our entire society than any other age group. They are represented in every socio-economic stratus, in every kind of neighborhood, in all of the ethnic and social groups and in every manner of settlement size and density from farm to metropolis. But even though the elderly reflect most of the general conditions prevailing in our society there are important differences that set them apart. Lower and fixed retirement income, loss of meaningful roles, loss of spouse and friends through illness and death, declining health, sensory capacity and mobility characterize the generally negative consequences of increased longevity which are not found in other age groups. The crucial point is that whereas basic human needs remain fairly constant across the life span, the appropriate means of meeting these needs vary generally by age group and specifically according to individual capacity.

With the knowledge that by the turn of the century there will be more than 30 million people in the United States 65 years of age and older has come the realization that there will be an increasing need for facilities to house older adults in the future. All of these considerations will play a part in the housing experiences of older individuals since the ability of a person to function within any environmental setting depends on his/her capabilities, as well as the characteristics of the setting. Thus, one of the difficulties of designing effective housing solutions for the elderly is that the circumstances, situations, and needs of the elderly vary greatly, and will be constantly undergoing a process of change over time.

Design, of course, goes beyond the mere physical dimensions of an appropriately configured and appointed space. It also has much to do with those more elusive qualities of autonomy, privacy, environmental mastery and sense of place. These more elusive qualities do not flow automatically from well designed physical spaces buy depend greatly on administration and staff. The attitude of staff and how it manages the delicate balance between residents' needs and the delivery of services can to a great extent determine the quality of life of those residents.

Design Issues

The first design issue has to do with the quality of the physical elements of the environment such as temperature-humidity levels, lighting and acoustics. It has been demonstrated for example, that certain temperature-humidity levels have a health impact. When humidity levels are below 30 percent as frequently happens in the winter when building are heated, there is a marked increase in the incidence of upper respiratory illnesses. This is a good example where good design and sensitivity to such issues by management can mean better health for the residents through keeping close track of humidity levels and making adjustments as called for within an accommodating environment.

Adequate lighting levels for activities of daily living must be part of an overall design for the building. It is known, for instance, that a given light level necessary to perform a given task doubles approximately every 13 years after the age of 25. Designers must be aware of the latest research regarding lighting arrangements and standards for older person and a knowledgeable staff must see to it that appropriate levels are actually used by replacing burned out light bulbs, replacing fixtures with those having the same capacity, as well as matching activities and appropriate lighting levels.

Acoustics is another area that needs informed design decisions. Background noise from air conditioners, appliances, television, and so on interferes with conversations and other forms of social interaction. Since presbycusis is a common age-specific hearing change attending the elderly (loss of hearing of high frequency sounds and decibel loss) it is important to specify the correct materials and surface treatments in order to better support activities of daily living. The primary design concept here is to eliminate noise and accentuate meaningful sounds.

Accessibility to buildings and within buildings must be assured for optimum use of buildings must be assured for optimum use of buildings and participation in programs and activities. Accessibility from parking areas and drop-off points should be barrier free and as close-by as possible. Connections between buildings should be covered and wheelchair accessible to facilitate neighboring and taking advantage of activities located beyond immediate living areas. And of course accessibility within a building to all the important activity areas such as dining, therapy and multiple use spaces should be part of the design as well.

With increasing problems of agility and balance, easy access between different areas in the living unit becomes more important for older person. Areas difficult to reach not only create inconveniences but can also be hazardous to residents' safety and well-being. However, easy physical access must not be achieved at the expense of visual privacy to areas such as bedrooms and bathrooms. To maintain their dignity with visitors, residents need to control visual access to areas where the more private activities such as personal hygiene and sleeping take place. As a result, careful consideration must be given to minimizing physical distance and barriers between public and private areas in the unit while maximizing visual privacy.

Visual impairments among the elderly is common and among the frail elderly even more common. Frequent difficulties encountered are with glare from uncontrolled natural light and from unbalanced artificial light sources; from lack of contrast between figure and ground; color changes and depth perception. Design solutions must include control of glare at the same time providing sufficient light; to provide strong contrast between lettering and background—preferably highly reflective lettering on a darker more absorptive background; avoiding blue and green colors in public areas as well as combinations of greens and blues on adjoining surfaces such as walls and floors; cueing stairs and other changes in walking surfaces to help overcome problems of depth perception.

Order and predictability of residential spaces, i.e., ease of finding desired destinations is important for elderly persons, particularly in larger more complex living arrangements. In design terms the goal is to organize spaces for their predictive value. The idea is that, in general, a space should be cued with landmarks which act as focal points for functionally different spaces. For example, surfaces can be color coded to visually signal functionally different spaces and, similarly, they can be textured for the tactile sense. The purpose is to load the spaces with sensory cues so that they may more effectively serve as points of reference and avoid ambiguous messages.

Safety and security always have high priority when living arrangements for the elderly are discussed. Such safety considerations as appliances that can be easily and safely operated;

stairways that are adequately lighted with secure handrails; stairs that are appropriately cued; safe and convenient bathing equipment and non-skid floor surfaces in the bathroom are only a few of the many safety elements in the residential environment that need to be provided. In terms of security the building must have reliable locks and bolts and whenever possible there should be 24 hour-a-day security personnel available along with an emergency system for each unit where assistance can be summoned when needed.

Storage and display space are also important design considerations. Older persons over their lifetime typically have accumulated many objects that reflect personal tastes and lifestyles. Some objects are still used, if only occasionally, and some object are associated with past events, persons, or periods in a long life. As older persons tend to reminisce, they place great value on these belongings and do not want to part with them. As a result, they need areas in the living unit to display as well as store their possessions. These items range from plants and photographs to suitcases and spare chairs and require a wide variety of display and storage areas. Problems of mobility and agility suggest that stored items be easily accessible and located closest to the area of their use.

Outdoor extensions of the living unit is a very positive feature and should be part of the overall design. Many older persons either by choice or physical limitation spend most of their time in their living units. With such a restricted home range, outdoor extensions of the private unit make on added importance. They provide a change of environment close at hand, an area to grown flowers and personalize, and they can perceptually increase the size of a living space. Outdoor extensions provide secure and protected environments for casual socializing with others. As a result, outdoor extensions such as patios and balconies are highly desirable. When provided they must meet residents' needs for privacy, and yet not compro-

mise residents' views of pathways and opportunities to social-
ize.

Likewise, there is a need to design larger social spaces
where residents with limited energies and capacities can still
meet and make new friends. Older residents often have no job
or immediate family to draw them into active community participation. As these former group ties weaken, older persons
become increasingly dependent on people in their residential
environment for social support and friendship. Older residents
also often find it difficult to go out of their way to make
friends. For these reasons older residents would benefit from
situations that provide opportunities to meet their neighbors
and other residents. Walking to, and taking part in, recreations
and community activities provide many opportunities for daily
social interaction. To achieve this, the activities center must be
located to maximize opportunities for meeting. This is especially true for housing sites where there is no off-site recreation
and commercial center within walking distance.

In addition to programmed spaces for socializing and gar-
dening, older persons have a need for more quiet and secluded
outdoor areas. They occasionally retreat to these areas when
they are in a contemplative mood, want to take a walk without
meting others, or need a change of scenery from their small
unit. An important aspect of retreats is that they offer additional choices to older residents. While the goal of a retreat
may be a nice quiet place, the process of getting there may be
just as important to older residents as the destination itself.

As indicated above older persons have special environmental needs that differ from those associated with other age
groups, although older residents themselves will often have
different background, life styles, and attitudes. Some environmental needs can be met by more responsive housing design.
Some design elements which must be better planned are small
details such as height and location of steps, type of doorknob,
location of electrical outlets and light switches. While it is true

that architects address such small scale elements in the final stages if a design, it is also true that if larger scale design issues fundamental to the whole conceptual design approach have not been responsive to older person's needs, the small elements will do little to make residents' lives more comfortable.

In the beginning of this chapter I made mention of some of the more elusive environmental qualities of autonomy, environmental mastery, privacy and sense of place. As I mentioned, these qualities do not flow automatically from design but depend greatly on the human or staff side of the environmental equation.

Spatial Experiences

Two years ago I completed a study with Dr. Valerie Polakow entitled *Life Space Over the Life Span*. In this study, we explored the spatial experiences of older people in a life review process in terms of how these memories and reminiscences shape the environmental perceptions of elderly residents living in perhaps their last home, a retirement center. We discovered when elderly residents traced their environmental biographies over a life-time, it yielded many insights into fundamental life theme of autonomy, privacy, solitude, environmental mastery and sense of place. When these themes are violated, as frequently occurs in living arrangements for the elderly, it is vital that we pay concerned attention to the changing relationship between the older person and his/her environmental context. This changing relationship is steeped in a life history of emotional attachment to place and a rich reminiscence of past possibilities of action. How does the legacy of living 80 or 90 years affect one's present environment perceptions and sense of well-being?

These are some of the questions we raised in exploring the environmental autobiographies with our informants. In listening to the stories of their everyday lives, the dramas, and the metaphors that have fashioned their spatial meanings, we realized that it is their voices that can best impact design as well as social and health personnel responsible for the humane management of people and space in planned residential settings.

Autonomy and Dependence

Living in a institutional setting promotes dependence or organizational rituals, restricts spatial and temporal autonomy and limits personal choices. Residents must eat prepared meals at specified times or forgo lunch or dinner. They are given no voice in the design of their rooms, or the inappropriately designed appliances—such as refrigerators that are too low, and central speakers that are too loud—or the inconvenience of getting out of bed and walking down a corridor to go the bathroom at night. Yet, paradoxically, once these residents report on a feeling of increased autonomy because barrier to mobility or fears of safety are lessened.

Mr. Jones describes how he used to want a larger room, but now as a stroke victim, confined to a walker, he appreciates the confining dimensions of his room. "But now I don't mind—I can go anywhere in the room with a cane—if the room was two feet bigger I couldn't make it without a walker."

For Mr. Jones the experience of living in a ready-made community far outweighs the necessary accommodations and surrender of personal control over his temporal and spatial landscape. For him, the environment is action—people centered, and, as he remarks "being busy keeps me alive."

Mr. Jones functions as an invaluable helper-of-others in this center and he, too, realizes the acute dilemma of many of the residents like himself.

"You get people who've been in houses with furnishings and you put them in a room smaller than this (he gestures at the size of his tiny room) and they've lived in a big house for 30 years—they've lost a husband or wife—they get pretty homesick—I try and help them—sometimes they lose their way—you can tell if they're lost by looking in their eyes— then I say come one, I'll take you *home.*"

It is clear, that Mr. Jones recognizes the center as home—for himself and many others—he is actively engaged in the world of the center having *disengaged* from life on the outside; for as he wisely points out, "I know it's not going to be better—but there's a lot I *can* do—here you've got people and you're not alone."

There were others living at the Center who did not feel their autonomy was affected at all. For instance, Mrs. McGregor tells us "I treat my room as an apartment. I come and go as I please, I invite visitors or not and I participate in those activities that interest me. Of course, one has to be firm sometimes about one's choices. The closeness of so many people can be a problem sometimes."

Being with others, engagement *in* the social world of the Center which stands outside the larger social world appears to foster opportunities for autonomy within a structure of dependence. At this point, the capacity to act on an transform one's given landscape becomes critical.

There is the need for fostering active participation on the part of residents, to the spatial landscape they have accommodated to, and accepted as their last *home.* Making it home, means also making it *mine.* How to facilitate and increase the sense of participation and personal autonomy is a challenge for designers of space as well as managers of space.

Privacy and Private Spaces

Privacy and private space as it was perceived by the study participants over their life time was most interesting.

Privacy was discussed in relationship to private space. Solitude was the primary focus. Most of the participants indicated that as children they did not have their own private room or space. They typically shared bedrooms with siblings. Mr. Smith said, "As long as I lived at home I never had my own room and always shared it with my brothers." Mrs. Smith made the observation that their younger siblings had such spaces after the older children in the family left home. It seems that the number of the children in the family and the birth order where very important when it came to having or not having a room of one's own—one's own private space. Mrs. McGregor reported that the bedroom remained her private space throughout her entire adult life until coming to the Retirement Center. She reports, "Even there my room is a bedroom so it seems natural to be sewing and writing and serving as a place of refuge just as it has done all my adult life."

Most of the participants as adults really did not have spaces that were exclusively theirs. Frequently, to attain a state of solitude, many participants said they went outdoors for long walks or would go to a nearby park. As children, most had to find private spaces out-of-doors to play or be alone. Mr. Smith indicated that as a child he remembers his house had one all purpose room, a kitchen, and bedrooms. If you wanted to play you went outdoors.

Privacy and Autonomy

Closely related to the issue of privacy is autonomy. Our society professes a fundamental belief in the uniqueness of the individual, in the basic dignity and worth as a human being. Social scientists have linked the development and maintenance of this sense of individuality to the need for autonomy—of not being manipulated or dominated wholly by others. Autonomy that privacy protects is vital to individual choice and is threatened by those who are not, for one reason or another, discretionary in their intrusion and usurpation of this choice. People in situations where they are dependent on others for their welfare are particularly vulnerable to losing their autonomy. There seems to be a general feeling among those who provide supportive services that the assistance being rendered compensates for the intrusion or loss of autonomy, a kind of "quid-pro-quo."

Other informants have very perceptive views on the subject. In terms of the living arrangements at the Center there is a range from independent cottages complete with kitchens, garages and yards to individual rooms which serve as sleeping and living rooms. Some of these rooms/units have toilets. Others do not. Thus the physical context within which the treatment of autonomy occurs is a very important environmental consideration.

Participants who lived in the detached cottages indicated they "liked it there rather than in the Center because we can pick and choose when to have company or see someone or not. We don't feel pressured to engage in programmed activities." "We feel the administration and staff should have more understanding of people's choices regarding the participation of activities with strangers." "At the Center, there is only a thin wall separating one life from another, here in this cottage we have several hundred yards. This distance has made it possible to have more choice."

The understanding of some of the participants of the role of the physical environment plays in maintaining one's autonomy is very perceptive indeed. There is also the understanding as observed by Mrs. Smith, that as one's health changes for the worse, "I may have to move to the Center and then I will have less to say about what one does, where one goes and who one sees."

Place Bonding and Displacement

As a person develops a sense of place over time, there are special meanings attached to activities and events which have a strong identification with a particular space(s) that may be characterized as place bonding. For example, a house in which a child grows up has many connotations of identity and if that person must involuntarily leave or if the house is destroyed, there is a profound sense of loss, the experience of displacement.

This was a theme articulated by some of the participants. For example, Mrs. McGregor observed, "We lost the farm during the Depression and long with it my walks along the river, the serenity of the trees and quiet places. I always enjoyed the out of doors." Mrs. Black indicated that, "My father developed a serious illness and as a result could not keep up with the demands of his position and was transferred to a less demanding situation and as a result lost the lovely house we lived in." Mrs. McGregor commented that "It was a lot easier for me to decide to come to the Retirement Center than some others because I didn't own my own house. I rented for a long time and so I didn't feel as attached as perhaps those might who owned their houses for a long time." Mr. Smith commented wistfully, "To be in the Upper Peninsula (Michigan), to enjoy the woods and the water, there's no place like it. That's my home, that's where I feel best, the big timber, the big country."

A sense of displacement seemed to be a common theme among our participants. Perhaps the most difficult displacement occurs when one enters a more sheltered situation. In most instances when people move to such a place it represents for the first time giving up one's home of long duration and accommodating to a different life style. This change represents more than giving up one's home, it frequently means giving up significant personal possessions. For example, Mrs. Black said, "I accumulated during the course of my adult life a number of possessions that had special meaning to me. For instance, I had a platform rocker that had been in my family for four generations. I played on it a great deal and I also sat in it and read in it as a child growing up. I also had a coin and stamp collection and a very unique collection of vases. When I came here I gave most of these and other things away because there really wasn't enough room here and I was afraid I'd lose them."

At the same time, possessions that are brought to the Retirement Center are frequently viewed as reminders of other times, events and places. They seem to provide tangible evidence of a meaningful past. As a person continues to age and the gap between the demands of the environment and the individual's competence widens, he or she begins to experience a loss of autonomy or mastery over necessary environmental elements to satisfy certain needs. As this gap widens, one's sphere of life-sustaining and life-enriching stimuli undergo a continuous reduction. At the same time, as more and more energy is expended in satisfying only the barest of life-sustaining needs one foregoes life-enhancing or life-enriching needs. It is vital that those who serve the frail elderly address the issue of how the physical environment can enrich or enhance personal growth.

Personal Growth

Personal growth is also related to the issue of adjustment in relocated from private housing to planned housing. People coming from private homes typically live in a single detached dwelling unit located on a lot that provides a spatial buffer in terms of proximity to others. Moving into planned housing presents a radical change since proximity is reduced, density is increased and the spatial buffer may not be any more than a thin wall. While there are a number of potentially positive elements in such a situation, an increased friendship pool, closer proximity and easier access to planned activities—not everyone can make the adjustment without help. More needs to be known in terms of what factors are involved in the adjustment process and how these may be applied to housing counselors and housing managers to assist in the successful adjustment of all residents to planned retirement housing.

It is difficult to separate design of physical spaces from management of physical space. This particularly true as it relates to the redesign of the institutional *time* frame, i.e., the scheduling and expectations of institutional rituals and program demands. These should be reexamined and made more flexible and individualized to more closely accommodated the diverse needs of residents in these special and planned environments.

Listening to the voices of informants indicates the great significance we should place on the environmental biography. It is within these symbolic meaning structures that current satisfaction/dissatisfaction needs can be located. Those who are concerned about the well-being of older persons can derive important metaphors with this approach which yield significant insights about the environments of elderly people and how best to design appropriate solutions.

In conclusion, housing is more than houses—it is the foundation upon which the essentials of life are anchored. Clearly, the quality of housing design can enhance or diminish the well-being of individuals and families as well as that of the entire community.

Bibliography

Christie, K. Four Federal Agencies Sign Agreement to Promote Better Design for Older Americans. News Release, National Endowment for the Arts, February 14, 1985.

Lawton, M.P. "An Ecological Theory of Aging Applied to Elderly Housing." *Journal of Architectural Education*, Vol. 31 (September 1977); pp. 8-10.

Pastalan, L.A. "The Physical Environment and the Emerging Nature of the Extended Care Model." In: Schneider, E.L., et. al. (editors). *The Teaching Nursing Home*. New York: Raven Press, pp. 19-85.

Pastalan, L.A. "Privacy as an Expression of Human Territoriality." In Pastalan, L.A.; Carson, D.H. (editors). *Spatial Behavior of Older People*. Ann Arbor: University of Michigan, 1970.

Pastalan, L.A.; Paulson, L.G. "Importance of the Physical Environments for Older People." *Journal of the American Geriatrics Society*, 1986.

Pastalan, L.A.; Polakow, V. "Life Space Over the Life Span." *Journal of Housing for the Elderly*, Vol. 4(1), (1986), pp. 73-85.

Pastalan, L.A. "Designing Housing Environments for the Elderly.: *Journal of Architectural Education*, Vol. 31 (September 1977), pp.11-13.

Pastalan, L.A.; Paulson, L.G. "Importance of the Physical Environments for Older People." *Journal of the American Geriatrics Society*, 1986.

Pastalan, L.A. "Environmental Design and Adaptation to the Visual Environment of the Elderly.: In: Sekuler, R., Kline,

D. and Dismukes, L. (editors), *Aging and Human Visual Foundation.* New York: Alan R. Less, 1982.

Sabin, T.D. "Biological Aspects of Falls and Mobility Limitations in the Elderly." *Journal of the American Geriatrics Society* (1982), p.51

Suransky, V.P. *The Erosion of Childhood.* Chicago: University of Chicago Press, 1982.

Tuan, Y. *Space and Place: The Perspective of Experience.* Minneapolis: University of Minnesota Press. 1977.

4

Segmenting the Market for Retirement Housing

by Morton Yulish, Susan B. Brecht, and
Howard K. Peters

Demographic Trends and Scenarios for Senior Housing Success

With each new article or speech touting the increase in the elderly population that will occur during the next decade and beyond, enthusiasm within the retirement housing industry builds. Based on the inevitable surge in the elderly population, it would seem that the retirement housing industry faces a boundless market. Yet, the retirement housing development community is becoming increasingly aware that this demographic growth will not automatically provoke an explosive demand for retirement housing.

As a result, the industry is more closely examining the potential market and realizing that the elderly are a diversified group of individuals with different ages, incomes, household types, health statuses, tenures, locations, ethnic backgrounds, life-styles and personal goals. All of these factors affect an individual's decision to move into a retirement housing community. We are also aware that traditional retirement housing facilities are just one of many living arrangements from which the elderly can choose.

The Census Bureau defines the elderly as individuals aged 65 and over. Initially, the retirement housing industry embraced this definition of the elderly market. Yet, most of the actual customers for mainstream retirement living products have been aged 75 and over. Recognizing this, the retirement housing industry redefined their market based upon the actual response to product. Most retirement communities have to reach those with middle-or upper-middle incomes, and the one-person female household has emerged as the primary customer.

While some slight differences may exist in the age of those moving into entrance fee facilities with lifecare versus rental facilities, most residents entering either type of retirement housing community are in their late 70s. Certain types of facilities have attracted more couples than is typical, but again, the norm is that couples will comprise no more than 25 percent of the initial resident base, and, as facilities age, this percentage is likely to decrease. Assisted living facilities are oriented toward a more frail, dependent resident and attract individuals in their early 80s. Again, one-person female households dominate the resident population.

Experience tells us that the elderly are not emerging as a broad, homogeneous market. Rather, much smaller segments of the market comprise the customer base of retirement housing. The most dominant target market segments have been one-person female households aged 75 and over and the husband-wife household aged 75 and over (a fairly distant second place). Depending upon whether a facility is entrance fee based or rental will further segment the above into their owner-renter counterparts.

The least likely candidates for retirement housing facilities are the one-person male head of household aged 75 and over and the census defined "Other," which often encompasses elderly siblings or unrelated individuals living together.

Having established the target market, we can examine the market potential in the retirement housing industry over the next five years. For the purpose of this analysis, we will assume that approximately 1,000 retirement communities currently exist, with an average of 150 units each yielding a total of 150,000 units. Overall vacancy is estimated at 10 percent. Five percent of the residents originated in households not headed by an elderly individual (for example, an elderly female living with her children). The balance are census-counted elderly households. We will estimate the population of retirement housing facilities to be:

- 70 percent one-person female heads of household aged 75+ with 1988 after-tax incomes ranging from $15,000 to $75,000

- 20 percent husband-wife households with same age and income characteristics

- 5 percent one-person male heads of household with same age and income characteristics

- 5 percent aged 65 to 74, one-person female, husband-wife or one-person male households with the same income characteristics

An annual income base of $15,000 was used, assuming that net proceeds from the sale of homes serves as an income offset and/or resource for an endowment/entrance fee. For this analysis, renters were also included.

Given these percentages, we developed a model that incorporates both National Planning Data Corporation's 1988 and 1993 elderly household estimates for the United States and Laventhol & Horwath's proprietary ElderCare Site Profile (ESP), which provides a detailed elderly market segmentation profile for a selected eight project specific market areas around the country. A more definitive analysis incorporating at least 100 such market areas is being planned for Laventhol & Horwath's 1990 study of the retirement housing industry.

Employing this model, we examined **four scenarios** that the retirement housing industry could follow between now and 1993. The first is based on the assumption that the current market share will not change and growth will solely be based on demographic changes that will occur by 1993:

Scenario A. Maintaining existing market share

Based upon the 1,000 facility/150,000 unit assumption and the age, income, and household type breakdown described above, we estimate the current market share—the percentage of age, income, and household type qualified households headed by a person age 75 and over estimated to be living in the 1,000 facility/150,000 unit retirement facilities—to be:

Market Segment	1988 Market Share
75+ One-Person Female Head of Households	14.60%
75+ Husband-Wife Households	2.50%
75+ One-Person Male Households	2.90%
Age 65 to 74 Households	0.14%

Assuming no change in market share, i.e., the retirement housing industry would be unable to draw a greater percentage of residents from each segment, the number of potential residents would increase by a sizeable amount solely due to demographic growth. Based only upon this growth and no increase in market share, we estimate a demand for almost 70,000 additional units (466 facilities, each with 150 units) by 1993.

However, turnover in the existing 1,000 facilities requires a considerable number of units to be filled during the next five years. Assuming a continued average occupancy rate of 90 percent and a turnover rate of 10 percent, approximately 13,500 units would have to be filled annually from the five-year demand of 70,000 additional units. Most of the increase generated from demographic growth, therefore, would be needed to sustain a 90 percent occupancy level. As a result, this scenario requires little expansion to the current supply of retirement housing facilities.

Scenario B. Increase in market share

Experience in the industry indicates a history of improved market share as the elderly become increasingly educated about retirement living alternatives. If the industry continues to demonstrate the success, value and desirability of retirement housing, some annual increase in market share would probably occur. Of course, the amount of growth would vary by individual markets.

Assuming that in addition to the demographic growth each market segment would demonstrate increased levels of interest, the following 1993 market shares were estimated to be:

Market Segment	1993 Market Share
75+ One-Person Female Head of Households	18.10%
75+ Husband-Wife Households	3.50%
75+ One-Person Male Households	3.20%
Age 65 to 74 Households	0.34%

These percentages reflect a five percent increase in market share through 1993. The five percent was proportionally allocated among the four household segments.

In addition to the 70,000 units filled by demographic growth, by 1993 Scenario B estimates that unit potential would increase by 69,000 units or 460 facilities. While this would indicate that growth is inevitable, it only addresses the industry's potential relating to the current customer profile. But there is significantly greater potential if the customer profile could be expanded.

Scenario C. Broadening market appeal to couples aged 75 and over

While couples currently comprise a small percentage of retirement housing residents-with the exception of lifecare-demographically they are a sizeable market segment. An increase in market appeal to elderly couples would generate a significant expansion to the market. In the retirement housing industry, housing options, such as life-style oriented condominiums, are currently being developed and may appeal more to elderly couples.

Scenario C assumes that increased interest in retirement housing facilities by elderly couples could expand market share by an additional five percentage points from 3.5 percent (Scenario B) to 8.5 percent by 1993. This increase adds approximately 80,000 units/553 facilities to the 69,000 units/460 facility growth generated from the first two scenarios. Combined, the estimated additional potential by 1993 would be 149,999 units/1,013 facilities.

The impact of broadening market appeal to husband-wife households aged 75 and over is considerable and illustrates the benefit derived from developing products that are more responsive to this sizeable market segment.

Individuals aged 65 to 74 comprise an even more substantial target market. In the past, the industry has experienced limited success in attracting these younger elderly to retirement housing communities. Scenario D addresses the potential impact of increasing the market share of aged 65 to 74 households.

Scenario D. Broadening market appeal to the aged 65 to 74 market

The younger elderly, while a tantalizing market segment, have proved to be elusive market for most health care oriented retirement living products. New approaches, such as the condominium leisure oriented community, must be found to increase appeal to this sizeable market segment.

In Scenario B, the potential 65 to 74 household market share in 1993 would be 0.34 percent. This represents a more than doubling of the Scenario A market share and was based upon an increase in the level of acceptance equal to the other segments.

However, if the aged 65 to 74 segment increases only at the same level as that of the more interested segments (one-person female head of households age 75 and over) an enormous market will be lost. Scenario D assumes that the industry can be more responsive to the desires of this massive market segment. While it does not assume as great an increase in market share as Scenario C did for husband-wife households, it does assume an increase by 1993 from .34 percent to 1.5 percent. This would generate the need for an additional 61,000 units/406 facilities by 1993. Should this market segment become active consumers of new retirement living opportunities, the potential for industry growth is vast given that each percent increase in market share represents numerous units.

These four scenarios offer significant opportunities for growth. The industry faces many options. We can continue to serve our mainstream constituency with mainstream products and keep existing retirement housing facilities fairly well occupied. We can continue to encourage our overall increase in market share by further educating our markets, filling existing market voids, and serving the residents well, thereby increasing our facility potential. We can seek greater penetration into the aged 75 and over husband-wife market segment and increase the potential for industry growth. And, if we are successful in reaching the younger elderly, the industry can dramatically expand. The industry, which clearly cannot expand without the interest of the elderly, can be versatile and committed to change and growth.

5

Financing Alternatives for Multifamily Retirement Housing

The Mortgage Bankers Association of America

Introduction

Finding and securing funds for retirement housing is more difficult and expensive than ever before. Although enlightened lenders, syndicators, and investors see the demographic trend that is resulting in an abundance of potential tenants, they are nonetheless aware of the overbuilding, workouts, and foreclosures that this industry has experienced in recent years. The elderly market has proven a sophisticated, elusive segment, and one of limited depth. Federal funding cuts have made government loan insurance hard to obtain. And developers must now conduct lengthy market studies and be armed with detailed pro formas to justify their projects to today's cautious lender.

Project pro formas for retirement housing must anticipate a long lease-up or sales period, with substantial allowances for operating deficits. In September 1988, a study reported in *Multi-Housing News* found that the average absorption rate was eight units per month for rental communities and "for sale" developments. Others have reported slower rates—in 1987, Laventhol & Horwath's Health Care Advisory service found that it typically takes between 19 and 24 months to fill a senior community.

Churches and religious organizations once dominated the retirement housing industry with life care communities financed by church funds, endowments, and bond issues. The U.S. Department of Housing and Urban Development (HUD) became a major source of funding and credit enhancement when it instituted programs to provide mortgage insurance for the construction and substantial rehabilitation of multifamily rental or cooperative housing projects. Private sector developers entered the retirement housing market in droves, drawn by favorable demographics and seemingly unlimited profit potential. From these entrepreneurial developers came the plethora of inventive vehicles available for financing retirement housing today.

This chapter examines some of these finance strategies, and provides an overview of popular financing methods. Keep in mind that financing methods and programs are changing. The Tax Reform Act of 1986 cleared a forest of financing alternatives, and a moratorium has been placed on the major HUD/FHA programs as this book goes to press. The optimal method of funding for your project will change with legislation, regulations, market conditions, and interest rates.

Tax Reform Complicates Financing

The Tax Reform Act of 1986

Financing multifamily housing of any type has become more difficult since Congress clamped down on tax incentives for real estate with the Tax Reform Act of 1986. This law eliminated the ability of most investors to use losses generated from real estate limited partnerships to shelter ordinary income from taxation. Prior to the Act, tax-exempt bonds, coupled with equity raised through limited partnerships, had been one of the most popular ways to finance senior housing. Both tools are now much less widely available, forcing developers to look for new sources of both debt and equity capital.

The Act placed strict limits on the use of tax-exempt bonds to finance housing, including overall volume limits on the issuance of bonds. The law outlined a new unified state per capita volume allocation system, defined the use of bond proceeds on qualifying uses, tightened the rules for renters benefiting from tax-exempt bond financing programs, and set forth new compliance rules. The Act imposes fewer limitations on tax-exempt bonds issued on behalf of not-for-profit sponsors.

Some see the changes as good news, since readily available financing may have encouraged development of projects not supported by market demand. Now, because of the Act, projects must be justified by solid market demand to obtain financing. While that may make things difficult for developers with limited resources and experience, it means less competition for those developers who can proceed with construction.

Sources of Equity

An important aspect of any real estate financial structure, equity is even more critical for senior housing because many lenders are unfamiliar with retirement project development and do not understand the risks involved. The simplest form of equity is a contribution of cash or land from the project sponsor or a joint venture partner. Other options include equity syndication through a limited partnership, or an equity investment from a real estate investment trust.

Most lenders will advise retirement housing developers not to consider applying for a loan unless they produce 20 to 25 percent of equity for the project. For most loans (especially now that FHA-insured mortgages are on hold), this is likely to remain the minimum acceptable level.

Some developers raise a portion of their equity requirement through entrance fees charged to residents or by pre-selling condominiums or shares in cooperatives; many states now regulate how entrance fees can be used to finance construction.

Distinctions between debt and equity blur as an increasing number of lenders take a participation in projects they finance, and as equity partners demand guaranteed returns. Project sponsors must dilute ownership of their projects to raise equity as well as debt. Thus, retirement housing deals begin to resemble joint ventures, whether they are actually structured that way or not. In fact, some observers think that the field will become increasingly dominated by large national firms with the resources and experience that lenders demand. Smaller firms attempting to build one or two projects may have little choice but to enter into a joint venture with such a firm.

Joint Ventures

A real estate joint venture is an association formed between a money participant and an established partner. A joint venture may take a variety of legal forms, including partnership, tenancy in common, or corporation. As in any partnership, each party to a retirement housing project must "bring something to the table." To form a successful arrangement, the company that controls a site will seek an organization with strong financial resources, special expertise in senior housing, and access to debt financing.

Before entering into a joint venture, each party should evaluate its short- and long-term goals to decide whether they are compatible with the proposed endeavor. The parties must agree, in writing, how they will share tax benefits and profits and losses, when cash flow will be distributed, who will be responsible for managing the partnership, and in what proportion each partner will make capital contributions.

In recent years, housing developers have found financial joint venture partners in savings and loans, insurance companies, and other financial institutions, although S&Ls have recently become more cautious about taking equity positions. Insurance companies may consider joint ventures, and usually opt for large projects.

Growing interest in the senior market has attracted other potential partners—churches and other not-for-profit organizations who employ a development firm to build on their land. Development firms have also turned to large health care providers as joint venture partners; hospitals have shown particular interest in such ventures.

Local developers may want to consider a joint venture with a stronger partner or a not-for-profit for several reasons:

- to gain control of or access to the project site;

- if they do not have strong financial resources;

- if they cannot personally guarantee a loan;

- if they cannot raise at least 20 percent equity;

- if there are no presales or preleasing;

- ■ if the prospective partner has a strong public image that would enhance market acceptance; or

- ■ if the prospective partner has senior housing management experience.

Equity Syndication

Syndication is the sale of equity interests in multifamily or commercial projects to investors, structured as a tax shelter with growth potential. Syndication provides equity capital, spreads risk, and allows the developer a disproportionate share of long-term capital gains upon eventual sale of the property.

Before the Tax Reform Act of 1986, syndication was an easy source of access to financing for housing developers, because it offered investors the best of three worlds: tax deductions, cash flow, and appreciation. Senior housing financed by syndication was especially attractive because investors would gain more tax deductions in early years. Then, once stabilized occupancy was reached, investors would have strong cash flow, especially if rents or fees for services were raised. Income would increase steadily, syndicators reasoned, since seniors would be reluctant to move even as rents or fees increased.

Prior to the Tax Reform Act, deductions from all types of real estate investments could be used to offset one's taxes on earned income or investment income. These losses included depreciation and deduction of construction period interest and taxes. Since most of the cost of a project was financed with debt, equity investors could often take deductions far in excess of their investment.

Today, senior housing syndications still boast income growth. These projects also continue to generate substantial tax losses for investors despite restrictions of the Tax Reform Act of 1986, but the Act has removed many tax incentives to build retirement housing. To compensate for the loss of those built-in tax benefits, syndicators must offer investors strong economic and cash returns. Some syndicators guarantee investors a specified rate of return and insist that the developer of the financed property back that pledge.

Syndication is a complicated and expensive process. Publicly offered partnerships must be registered with the Securities and Exchange Commission and often involve front end fees of 20 to 30 percent of the money raised. Private partnerships are less complex, but can be marketed only to investors who meet minimum net worth and income requirements.

Real Estate Investment Trusts

Real estate investment trusts (REITs) are corporations, associations, or trusts in which one or more trustees who control acquisitions and investments (much like mutual fund portfolio managers) hold title to real estate assets or funds for real estate investments. REITs offer publicly traded shares in corporations specializing in all types of real estate investments.

While limited partnership investments were hurt by the Tax Reform Act, REITs have become more attractive. The 1986 law relaxed some of the restrictions on REITs, and they do not have to compete with tax-oriented partnerships for properties. Equity-oriented REITs (as opposed to those that make mortgage loans) are especially popular now, and many of them take equity positions in retirement housing, often on an unleveraged basis.

Sources of Debt Financing

Conventional financing sources for retirement housing include commercial banks, insurance companies, and pension funds. Other debt financing sources include taxable and tax-exempt bonds (to the extent they can still be used), and real estate investment trusts that make mortgage loans. Most lenders are interested in senior housing but cautious in their approach to specific projects. Developers must work hard to convince private financiers to make a loan, even on conservative terms and conditions.

Commercial banks have increased their interest in retirement housing and have been the primary source of construction financing for retirement facilities, usually making loans with interest rates that float with the prime rate. When it comes to permanent financing, however, most banks remain cautious and slow to make commitments.

Overbuilding in commercial office markets has bolstered the interest of insurance companies in housing, but it remains to be seen whether these companies want the added risk of financing retirement housing on a large scale. Insurance companies generally look for large loans, a limitation that will preclude many smaller retirement properties from finding financing. Loans by insurance companies are likely to be for shorter terms with loan-to-value ratios of no more than 75 or 80 percent. Many insurance companies will also insist on a participation in cash flow and residuals before approving a loan.

While savings institutions such as savings and loan associations and mutual savings banks have long been the single most important source of financing for regular multifamily rental projects, developers will find that these lenders are frequently unfamiliar with the elderly housing industry and will require a basic education on the topic before they will fund service-oriented senior housing.

Whatever the type of lender, developers must have a submission package that includes a highly detailed and credible market study. Further, they must demonstrate that at least some members of their development team have experience with senior housing. Even then, lenders will probably make permanent loans for no more than 75 to 85 percent of value, with adjustable interest rates or a participation in the cash flow and residuals of the property. Many lenders will not make loans with terms of more than 10 years based on 30- to 40-year amortization schedules.

If lenders are considering providing construction financing for condominiums or cooperatives aimed at seniors, they will want evidence of a substantial number of presales before they will approve the loan.

The type of permanent loan structures will vary by lender but may include adjustable rate loans that float at one to three points above an index. Loan terms are usually in the seven- to ten-year range based on 25- to 30-year amortization schedules. Another loan structure is the graduated payment or negative amortization mortgage. A portion of the interest due in the first years of a loan is added to the unpaid principal balance. Thus, payments start low and increase to the required level over several years as project income increases. Savings and loans also make participating mortgages in which they offer an attractive permanent loan rate in return for a 10 to 50 percent share of cash flow, plus residuals upon eventual sale of the property.

Participating Mortgage Funds

Rental retirement facilities can obtain debt financing from partnerships formed to make participating mortgage loans. During the first half of 1988, interest rates on these programs were in the 9 to 9.25 percent range, plus an annual mortgage insurance premium of 0.75 percent. Typically, the lender demands at least 25 percent of cash flow and residual value.

Tax-Exempt Bonds

Historically, tax-exempt bonds were the prevailing vehicle to finance senior housing, offering a percentage rate averaging two points below taxable market rates. Tax-exempt issues result in lower debt service, as well as not-for-profit credibility in marketing to seniors, a high level of acceptance to conventional lenders, a longer amortization period, and flexible loan periods of five to 40 years.

However, tax-exempt bonds have negative features. For example, they take four to six months to obtain, are dependent upon political decisions, and require high up-front fees and legal costs. The legislative trend is to require more qualifications for tax-exempt bonds, which means more paperwork.

In addition, the Tax Reform Act placed strict low-income occupancy requirements on tax-exempt bond-financed housing. Now, for-profit sponsors have to reserve a certain proportion of the units for low-income persons. The use restriction obligations end after 15 years, or upon repayment of the bonds, whichever comes later.

These changes, plus many more technical changes, have made bond financing unattractive to most project sponsors. However, if interest rates on conventional financing rise substantially, the lower interest rates available through tax-exempt bond financing may offer debt service savings sufficient to compensate for the new restrictions. Tax-exempt bonds are still an option, but one that involves many different players, political decisions, and higher up-front fees and legal costs than certain of the forementioned alternatives.

Issue costs for tax-exempt bonds include the following fees:

- bond counsel;
- depository trust company;
- issuer;
- loan origination points;
- printing - bonds;
- printing - statements;
- rating agency;

- surety;

- trustee;

- underwriter's counsel;

- underwriter's discount.

Annual costs for tax-exempt issues include the following fees:

- indexing agent;

- issue fees;

- lender;

- trustee.

Taxable Bonds

Taxable or market rate bonds have none of the requirements for family size adjustments or low income set-aside restrictions of tax-exempt bonds. The steps involved in obtaining taxable financing are similar to those for tax-exempt bonds.

Taxable bonds carry none of the restrictions of tax-exempt bonds, but, like tax-exempt bonds, they involve up-front issuance costs of including six to nine discount points. If a bond is publicly offered, the sponsor must obtain letters of credit or bond insurance to obtain the best possible credit rating and therefore the lowest possible rate of interest. The borrower would also have to pay the cost of a letter of credit to secure an AAA rating. Taxable bond issues carry higher yields than tax-exempt issues. Spreads range from 30 basis points over U.S. Treasuries for high quality issues to 150 to 200 basis points over for lower rated issues.

Market rate or taxable bonds offer other advantages:

- quicker funding decisions;

- fewer government requirements;

- fewer costs of complying with government regulations;

- flexibility;

- stability of funding.

Forms of taxable bonds include:

- capital appreciation bond;

- convertible capital appreciation bond;

- tender option bond;

- private placement bond;

- variable rate demand bond;

- revenue, appreciation payment and principal repayment bonds.

Mortgage Rate

The mortgage rate varies with the market, current or changing legislation, and risk. Whatever type of bond issue used, the final mortgage rate is calculated as follows:

bond rate + liquidity guarantees + fees = mortgage rate

"Fees" may include a lender fee, trustee fee including collateral fee, re-marketing agent fee, and a servicing fee for government programs.

Real Estate Investment Trusts

Retirement housing, nursing homes, and health care facilities have recently become the hottest targets for investment by REITs. This is part of the trend toward securitization of real estate. Like partnerships, REITs "pass through" income and losses to shareholders (instead of partners). REITs are traded like stocks and equities, giving small investors a way to invest in a diversified real estate portfolio with full liquidity.

Like other lenders, REITs make short-term loans with low loan-to-value ratios and take participations in retirement housing projects. The National Council on Seniors Housing of the National Association of Home Builders reported that in 1988 the typical REIT loan had a 7- to 10-year term with a balloon payment based on a 30-year amortization. For example, one REIT offered a rate of 10 percent, with a participation of 50 percent, and a discount of two points.

Developers or lenders may structure an REIT to raise capital for mortgages on a small number of specified properties. An REIT can be closed-ended, meaning that no additional shares can be offered after the initial offering, or open-ended, meaning additional shares can be issued in the future.

Credit Enhancements

Credit enhancements provide additional security to lenders and investors, providing assurance other than future project revenues, and are necessary to obtain long-term financing. They speed the funding process, and lower the bond rating, interest rate charged, and required equity contribution.

Credit enhancement vehicles include:

- equity contributions;
- letters of credit;

- collateralized letters of credit;
- surety/insurance programs;
- combination letter of credit and insurance program;
- escrow bonds;
- pooled programs/REIT;
- direct developer guarantee;
- guaranteed investment contracts;
- Fannie Mae programs;
- Ginnie Mae programs;
- interest rate swaps;
- entrance fees.

Credit enhancements a developer used to secure bond financing will incur highly variable up-front costs. Up-front costs of credit enhancements may include:

- lender's fee;
- surety premium;
- cost of insurance;
- underwriter discount;
- program fee;
- issuer fee.

Tax Credits For Low-Income Housing

Development of low-income housing for the elderly and others is encouraged under the Tax Reform Act of 1986. The Act authorized a tax credit that investors in low-income housing projects may use to offset their tax liability. Investors may offset taxes on up to $25,000 of income, whether that income is defined as active or passive under the tax code, by claiming the low-income housing tax credit. For new construction and rehabilitation projects, the amount of the credit is nine percent of the portion of the cost of the project that is attributable to low-income occupancy. For acquisition of a project, or construction or rehabilitation of a project that will also receive a federal subsidy, the amount of the credit is four percent of that portion of project costs attributable to low-income occupancy. Investors may take the credit annually for 10 years, but projects for which the credit is taken must continue to house eligible low-income households for at least 15 years.

To qualify as low-income housing for the credit, a project must have 20 percent of the units designated for occupancy by persons earning no more than 50 percent of the area median income, or 40 percent of the units for persons earning up to 60 percent of the area median income.

Conclusion

Retirement housing is a complex subject for both lenders and project sponsors. Though demographic trends point to a strong and increasing demand for such housing, neither developers nor lenders fully understand how to tap this market. All parties to the development process must be cautious in underwriting, appraising, and analyzing the feasibility of retirement projects.

Developers and lenders must continue to test the depth of the market to gain the experience they need to reduce the risk of senior housing, and make financing such projects as routine as long-term, self-amortizing home mortgages.

An important thing to remember about the senior market is that it is not homogeneous. Every senior has different goals, preferences, and constraints regarding their housing choices. Developers and lenders who fail to understand that and build for a stereotypical "senior citizen" are unlikely to succeed.

Sources

Elderly Housing Options: Putting Together a Cost Effective Development and Planning Process. Scott, Terence J. and Robert F. Maziarka, Pluribus Press, Chicago, 1987.

Seniors Housing; A Development and Management Handbook. The National Association of Home Builders, NAHB Press, Washington, 1987.

Financing Income-Producing Real Estate. Stevenson, Eric. McGraw-Hill, Inc., 1988.

Special thanks to Jim Sherman of Laventhol & Horwath Health Care Consulting for his contributions to this chapter.

6

Selection of the Development Team and Management Team

by Alan Scott

Senior housing project failures are often linked to an inexperienced development team. The careful selection of a skilled, qualified team may be the best insurance policy for risk minimization. The investment of up-front capital to assemble a qualified team will pay large dividends in the successful development of senior housing. However, the rather limited supply of capable, competent professionals may make the selection process challenging.

The following discussion is an analysis of the criteria for the selection of development team members. The person tasked with team selection must remember that project success is dependent upon a group effort that blends the critical elements of conception, design, finance, construction, sales, marketing, and management. The process consists of the following steps:

- Definition of disciplines/positions required;
- identification of potential team members;
- establishment of criteria for selection;
- definition of levels of service and desired results;
- negotiation of fees and terms;
- contractual arrangements—Letter of Understanding;
- coordination and oversight.

Definition of Positions Required

The type of senior housing and level of care dictates the size and type of development team. The most basic structure of a senior housing development team includes those shown in Figure 1.

The team quarterback is typically the developer—he is often responsible for team selection. While the developer is usually the leader, it is critical that his plans, objectives, and goals be shared with each team member. Each player should participate in the decision making process to capitalize on each member's valuable knowledge and experience.

Figure 1. Development Team for Senior Housing Project

Identification of Potential Team Members

Selection of team members is often hampered by a shortage of experienced professionals. With research and desire, you can locate qualified team members. Consider the following options for the search:

1. **Locate and analyze successful projects.** There are many success stories in senior housing. To find thriving facilities, contact area builders, senior centers, area senior projects, regulatory agencies such as HUD and State Department of Health, and senior housing professionals. Determine the strengths and weaknesses of the development team members, and the facility itself. Who was the architect who designed the efficient project, within budget, and was most sensitive to seniors' needs? Who was the best interior designer? What attributes make this management team successful? Remember that your goal is to recruit those people who were instrumental to the facility's success.

2. **Contact associations.** The following associations feature national senior housing talent, products and services:

    - National Association of Home Builders (Senior Housing Council)
    - American Association of Retired Persons
    - American Association of Homes for the Aging
    - National Association of Senior Living Industries
    - National Council on Aging

3. **Network.** National senior housing consultants are an invaluable source for qualified, experienced professionals.

4. **Read industry publications and literature.** Articles including names of senior housing specialists can often be found in such trade magazines as:

   - Builder Magazine

   - Multi-Housing News, Senior Living Section

   - Professional Builder

   - Long-Term Care

   - Modern Maturity

   - Ram Digest

Criteria for Selection

The selector should consider the following qualifications and personality traits when interviewing potential team members:

1. **Sensitivity.** Sensitivity to seniors' emotional, physical, and psychological needs are critical for understanding the planned lifestyle for residents. Each team member must be sympathetic to the needs of the senior population—such basic needs as independence, security, privacy, and convenience.

2. **Experience.** Senior housing experience is a must. Lack of experience among team members is a major contributing factor to failure, and an experienced development team will make it easier to obtain financing. Previous exposure to success (or even failure)

allows the team to adopt successful components and discard features of failed projects.

3. **Compatibility.** To facilitate a smooth transition from project concept to reality and team cohesiveness and efficient and timely decision making, a proper balance must be present of personalities must be present. Flexibility, compassion, and team spirit, and a clear understanding of goals and objectives will motivate the team to perform.

4. **Resources.** Each member must allocate the necessary human and financial resources to the project to accomplish goals and objectives in a timely manner, within budget. A "weak link" on the team will tax the energy of other members. Failure of one or more team members can negatively influence the entire team. It is the responsibility of the team coordinator to assure that each team member has the manpower and financial resources necessary to perform their assigned duties.

5. **Financial Considerations.** Unfortunately, budgetary constraints are often the leading criteria in selection of team members, downplaying such important qualifications as experience. Dollars invested in qualified team members are well spent. Budget, fee structure, payment schedules and additional service fees need to be considered. A clear definition of responsibility and level of service required will aid in identifying adequate compensation. Among qualified, experienced professionals, there is pricing consistency. Management fees, for example, are often based on a percentage of adjusted gross income which typically ranges from 4 to 6 percent.

6. **Knowledge.** Familiarity with the local area is beneficial. Even experienced professionals may be ignorant of local conditions such as building and zoning codes, and characteristics of the local marketplace. Experienced, qualified professionals with knowledge of the local market can be a blessing to a development team, and may even save money. This person will often speed the approval processes.

7. **Creativity.** In senior housing, a specific product is designed for a specific market. Multi-levels of care in each project are targeted to specific markets for each level of care. Competition in senior housing is proliferating. The ability of the team to plan a creative, and on-budget development will increase the chance for success. Stale, institutional design, (and conversely, an overly designed product), may be detrimental.

8. **Strengths and weaknesses.** It is of critical importance for the team coordinator to recognize exploitable strengths and weaknesses in each team member. A combination of team members with compatible and complimentary strengths will enhance decision making processes.

9. **Verification.** Validate information obtained during the interview and selection process. The following are steps one should take in the verification process:

   - Check with references and clients to confirm perceptions of the candidate, both positive and negative;

   - confirm any claimed designation with the certifying agency;

- review and assess financial statements of the team member to ensure the presence of adequate resources;

- visit the potential member's place of business and confirm that adequate human resources, facilities and systems exist;

- review examples of work samples performed by the professional to ensure high standards;

- verify that awards claimed were actually received;

- visit projects that were planned, designed, built, marketed or managed by the candidate and observe firsthand the quality of service provided. Discussions with the residents and staff can be most helpful to uncover hidden problems or mistakes.

Definition of Levels of Service/Duties Required

A clear understanding of what is expected of each member and a knowledge of desired results will bolster a team's cohesiveness. Short-and long-term strategies should be formulated at the outset. Typical services are shown in Figure 2.

The establishment of clear, concise, specific goals and objectives for each professional is essential to achieve the desired results. This section illustrates the importance of goals and objectives of each team member.

Figure 2. Typical Services Performed by Team Members

Team Member	Typical Service Options
Builder/ Developer	General Contracting
	Project Scheduling
	Project Coordination
	Construction Management
	Selection of Development Team
	Design Services
	Feasibility Analysis
	Code Audits
	Contract Negotiations
	Secure Financing
	Lender Coordination
	Job Reporting
	Cost Estimation
Market Analyst	Demographic Analysis & Projections
	Verification of Service & Amenities
	Feasibility Analysis
	Telemarketing Surveys
	Questionnaires
	Strategic Planning
	Product Positioning
	Quantitative Surveys
	Focus Groups
	Development of Marketing Strategy

Figure 2. Typical Services Performed by Team Members (continued)

Team Member	Typical Service Options
Market Analyst	Competitive Analysis
	Conceptual Planning
	Site Evaluation
	Development of Marketing Plan
	Financial Planning
	Appraisals
	Demand Analysis
	Operations Forecast
	Tax Effect Forecast
	Capital Financing
	Market Projections
	Absorption Analysis
Architect/ Engineer	Design Specifications
	Basic Design
	Structural Engineering
	Mechanical Engineering
	Electrical Engineering
	Landscape Planning
	Civil Engineering
	Soils Engineering
	Site Planning
	Cost Estimation
	Feasibility Studies
	Interior Design
	Code Compliance Audit
	Traffic Analysis
	Exterior Colorization

Team Member	Typical Service Options
Architect/ Engineer	Graphics Design Environmental Studies Project Scheduling Government Approvals Contract Negotiation Construction Management Construction Draws Space Management Energy Management/Analysis Product Evaluation
Interior Designer	Design Consultation Graphics and Signage Exterior Colorization Architectural Element Analysis Furniture Artwork and Accessory Selection Color Boards Space Planning Budgeting Leasing/Sales Design Supervision of Installations Product Specification Furniture Layout Plan Review and Design Purchasing Services
Gerontologist	Sensitivity Analysis Market Analysis Product Specification Management Consulting Marketing Consulting

Figure 2. Typical Services Performed by Team Members (continued)

Team Member	Typical Service Options
Gerontologist	C.O.N. Consulting
	Focus Groups
	Product Positioning
	Operations Analysis
	Human Performance Analysis
	Program Analysis
Lender	Feasibility Analysis
	Financial Underwriting
	Capital Sources
	Construction Inspections
	Actuarial Studies
	Budget Reviews
	Financial Options Analysis
	Financial Brokerage
	Provision of Credit Enhancement
Marketing Consultant	Develop Marketing Plan
	Establishment of Pre-Sales
	Pre-Lease Program
	Design Outreach Program
	Sales and Lease Retention Program
	Staff Recruitment
	Sales Conferences & Training Seminars
	Market Analysis
	Public Relations
	Newsletter Preparation
	Community Planning

Team Member	Typical Service Options
Marketing Consultant	Focus Groups/Consumer Surveys Market Testing Development of Service and Amenity Package Absorption Analysis Media Planning Promotion Planning Special Events Establish Sale/Leasing Program Establish Follow-Up System Marketing Implementation Prospect Analysis Product Evaluation Product Specifications Development of Budgets

Manager	Staff Recruiting
	Job Descriptions
	Budgeting
	Ongoing Management Operations
	Interdisciplinary Coordination
	Bookkeeping/Accounting
	Tenant Selection
	Lease Enforcement
	Social, Educational and
	  Recreational Programming
	Development of Procedures
	  Manual
	Implementation of Outreach
	  Program
	Counseling Services
	Maintenance Programming

Figure 2. Typical Services Performed by Team Members (continued)

Team Member	Typical Service Options
Manager	Development of Service Package
	Purchasing Services
	Rent Collection
	Insurance Analysis
	Policy Making
	Case Management
	Resident Surveys
	Reporting
	Handling of Service Packages
	Regulatory Interaction
	Purchase of Materials

Architect

Architectural design must be in harmony with surrounding neighborhoods. Environments must be designed to satisfy the needs of senior adults, and the social, physical and psychological changes they undergo. Every feature must be designed with comfort and convenience in mind. Integration of multi-levels of care in one community requires an architect or team of architects specialized in each level of care. The goals and objectives of the architect are:

- To design a cost-efficient project, offering an aesthetically pleasing environment that satisfies the operational needs of, and is accepted by, the target market;

- design flexibility to accommodate aging-in-place and programmatic changes;

- maximization of construction dollar;

- implementation of the Architectural Design Checklist (Figure V), as prepared by the development team;

- efficient and attractive design, both internally and externally.

Require that the most capable architect on staff be on the job during negotiations, and that he design a specific product for a specific use—no "cookie cutter" blueprints. The design philosophy of Walter Zaremba, Sr., an "old-time" builder, has proven successful—"Keep it simple, economical, and beautiful."

Market Analyst

There are several schools of thought on the analysis of the senior housing market that focus on a few key statistics such as number of movers, penetration rates, and vacancy rates. **A misreading of the potential market is the number one cause for**

new project failure. Market studies serve as a foundation for decision making by planning and zoning bodies, lenders, architects, land planners, interior decorators, marketing staff and management staff. Specific goals and objectives may include the following:

- Verification of site location;

- verification of project amenities offered;

- confirmation that unit design meets the target market;

- confirmation of a realistic, achievable absorption projection;

- assistance in positioning product in the marketplace;

- careful assessment of competition and inventory analysis;

- minimization of development risk;

- confirmation that an adequate target market exists;

- verification of unit mix and project size;

- verification that rent structure can be supported by target market;

- assessment of buyer profile;

- development of pricing strategies.

An experienced, qualified senior market analyst will not hesitate to recommend abandonment of a project if a market will not support it. Hiring a qualified market analyst with a significant database in the project marketplace will save time, money and effort.

Interior Designer

Designing lifestyle environments for seniors requires a keen awareness of health, safety, functionality, and aesthetics. An understanding of physical impairments is critical. For example, the yellowing and thickness of eye lenses as one ages may result in altered perceptions of color, false depth perception, and loss of equilibrium. Interior design for seniors should consider the following goals and objectives:

- Imaginative, eye-appealing interiors will increase sales or lease contracts;

- living environments that reflect some nostalgic aspects of design will help seniors adjust more readily to their new environment;

- designs must offer independence, privacy, comfort, and a sense of personal identity for the residents.

Gerontologist

Designing, marketing, and managing spaces for an aging population with special needs demands consultation with a gerontologist. Identification of the needs of the senior market and following developments and research findings in gerontology is essential.

Gerontologists help to ensure a high quality living environment for the resident, and to increase the marketability of the project by the incorporation of design elements which cater to the needs of an aging resident.

A common problem in the senior housing industry is the failure to adequately assess the market before the facility is designed and constructed. Failure to consider the limitations that old age imposes, such as hearing loss, and loss of sight and motor control will damage the marketability of the project, as will a lack of understanding of the living patterns of the aging market. A gerontologist's input into the design, marketing, and management program is invaluable to assure that the project is in harmony with the taste of the market.

Lender

The lender is typically the least understanding player in the relatively new senior housing industry. Many lenders have declined financing to senior housing projects for such reasons as the single purpose use and business versus investment, long lease-up periods and high operating deficits. As the senior housing field grows, many lenders realize the vast opportunities in this field. Some goals and objectives to consider are:

- Utilization of a financing vehicle that offers a reasonable rate, and rate of return to investors;

- flexibility in pay-in schedule to accommodate a lower pay-in rate in earlier years, to overcome the substantial initial operating deficits that may occur early in the life of a project.

There are myriad financing vehicles available for senior housing, including conventional, institutional, federal enhancement, and bond financing, all of which can be creatively structured. Select a lender experienced in senior housing, that allows flexibility in the creation of a financing program mix.

Marketing Specialist

The adage that, "The three most important factors leading to the success of a housing development are location, location, and location." does not apply to senior housing projects. Location, marketing, and management are the important variables in this highly competitive industry.

Special skills and education are required to market to seniors; poor marketing is a common blunder in retirement housing. For example, an intense and expensive newspaper advertising campaign will likely yield fewer prospects than a less expensive direct mail effort. Marketing efforts must begin at the idea stage, and must be considered in every stage of project development. Seniors will require multiple visits and take months, sometimes years, before deciding whether to move. Therefore, a pre-marketing campaign is important to generate prospects well before a project is ready for move-in.

A marketing specialist will prove helpful in the development and implementation of a successful pre-marketing, marketing, and post-marketing campaign. These efforts help to achieve full occupancy at desired rent or sales prices, in the minimum possible time, preventing or lessening operating deficits. The bottom line: The owner gets paid when occupancy exceeds break-even to net income.

The National Assocation of Home Builders National Council on Seniors Housing provides extensive courses in education and certification in senior housing marketing, a highly recommended course for anyone involved in the marketing of retirement projects.

The following exhibit illustrates a typical marketing plan for a development.

Management

Due to the unique nature of the senior market, management requires specialization. Residents are often more concerned with the social, recreational, and educational programs and services available than with the dwelling unit itself. As services play an even larger role, as in the case of congregate housing and assisted living, the duties and responsibilities of management increase. The management approach to this form of living is similar to that of a full service hotel, with a social service program.

Figure 3. Seniors Rental Marketing Plan, Month 1

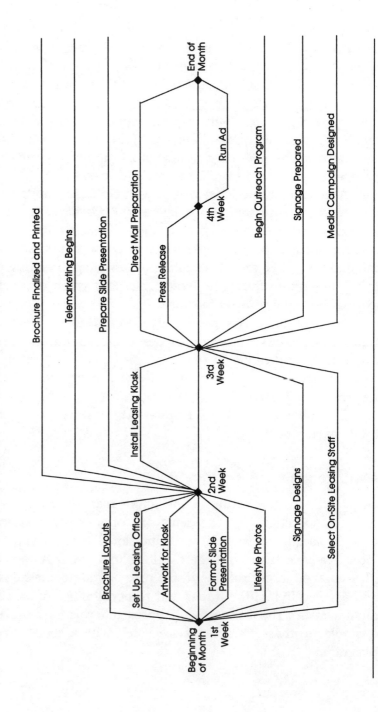

Management should hire a staff that is sensitive to the emotional, physical, and psychological needs of the elderly—those traits are critical to maintain a high percentage of resident retention. Further, management should strive for full occupancy, and maintain vigilant oversight of the physical plant.

Negotiation of Fees and Terms

Fees must always be negotiated up front. Accurate budgeting mandates precise measurement of costs before work begins. Project planning expenses are difficult to estimate. Experienced professionals can offer invaluable assistance in determining costs, including the cost of their own services. Figure 4 illustrates typical fee structures.

Fee structures vary widely according to the area, type of projects, competition, and experience level, and should be negotiated on a "job activity basis" to allow flexibility in the event of mid-stream service level changes. Compensation will vary widely, based largely on the scope of work to be performed. It is therefore imperative that a specific, well-defined scope of work is established.

Beware hidden costs. For example, blueprinting charges in an architect's contract are rarely specified and only identified as a reimbursable cost. Shocking news may arrive when the initial invoice is received for blueprint charges which may be double or triple the rate currently paid. Hidden costs can include travel expenses, hourly work, secretarial charges, change orders due to plan deviations, and graphics.

Projects are only as good as the human resources allocated to them. The most qualified individual must be the team representative, responsible for coordinating all efforts.

Figure 4. Typical Fee Structures

Builder	Five to seven percent of hard costs and two percent builder overhead, plus 10%-15% on additional services.
Developer	Three to five percent of total costs
Market Analyst	$1,000 to $3,000 per diem consulting rate. $5,000 to $15,000 for market study. $10,000 to $15,000 for focus groups.
Architect	One to four percent of hard costs, depending on size of project/price per unit. Fee broken down by level of service.
Civil Engineer	Fee of $20.00 to $50.00 per unit, additional fees by established hourly rate. $75.00 to $125.00 per unit.
Interior Designer	$2,000 to $5,000 per floor plan, 10% to 15% mark-up on purchases.
Gerontologist	Hourly or per diem fee, or fixed fee per project.
Lender	Conventional loan, One to three points, one percent brokerage fee, one percent lender fee, three and one-half percent on FHA deals.
Marketing Consultant	$1,000 to $3,000 per diem, fixed fee per activity.
Property Manager	Four to five percent of effective gross income. Often has incentive clause for additional fee when projected occupancy of cash flow levels is exceeded. Percentage of equity in troubled projects.

Contractual Arrangements

The contract serves as a recapitulation of all negotiations including scope of work, fee structure, terms, and optional services. It is advisable to follow up verbal negotiations with a "Memorandum of Understanding" which serves as the basic agreement and becomes the foundation of the contract. Revisions are costly; a complete contract will hold revisions to a minimum. The contractual agreement must always include the correct name and address of each party, and terms of payment.

Coordination and Oversight

A successful project is a combination of hard work, team effort, property coordination and oversight. Coordination involves:

- Pre-construction development activities;

- coordination of construction activities;

- implementation of a strategic marketing plan;

- implementation of a management plan.

The scheduling of activities is influenced by the type of development, and source and type of financing. The development of and marketing and management process for a multi-level life care community is very different from that of a single family retirement community. Similarly, the financing a project with a conventional loan will be differ greatly from financing with the rigid requirements of tax-exempt bonds coupled with HUD 221(d)4 mortgage insurance, and a pension fund equity partner. Conditional and firm commitment requirements, compliance with prevailing wage rates and FHA minimum property standards, and environmental clearances are only a few of the HUD requirements that complicate coordination and scheduling.

Construction activities are typically coordinated through a general contractor or construction management team with periodic owner, lender, and investor inspection for verification and review purposes. Most general contractors provide field supervision and a project manager, and subcontract work out to the trades. A developer who hires an outside general contractor will often hire a project or construction manager to monitor the activities of the general contractor and subcontractors.

Many different scheduling types are used on the job sites, including commonly used critical path method (CPM) charts, bar charts, and grid charts. Whatever method used should be a simple tool, easily read and understood. CPMs are frequently cleverly constructed but misunderstood by users.

The strategic marketing plan is often broken down into both pre-lease-up activities and ongoing marketing activities. Pre-lease-up activities are a key factor on the list of reasons for success or failure. The timing of these activities is sensitive it must not be too early or late. Typical pre-marketing of rental communities starts six to nine months before lease-up. For-sale communities often start one to two years prior to construction.

Careful coordination and monitoring of marketing and management activities is essential to the ongoing success of any project.

Conclusion

The future of senior housing will be a direct result of the success of today's development teams, their competency and effectiveness, and understanding of this largely need-driven market. The careful definition of desired players, negotiation of fees, terms and contracts, and finally coordination and oversight will go far to ensure project success. The selection of those people who make senior projects work can be a long, complex process. If the team selection procedure emulates the methods outlined in this chapter, it may be a rewarding process as well.

Figure 5. Architectural Design Checklist
Retirement Housing

Project Name:_____ Date:_____ Prepared By:_____

A. Overall Building Requirements:

Configuration: Atrium_____ Center Corridors_____ Flats_____
No. Stories_____

Architectural Style: Colonial_____   Contemporary_____
Mansard_____   French Provincial____
English Tudor____   Cape Cod____
Traditional____   Other____

Exterior Treatment: Brick_____   Wood_____
Aluminum_____   Vinyl____
Stone____   Stucco____

B. Common Area Building Requirements:

Room	Size (SF)	Finish Floor	Wall
Commercial Kitchen	_____	_____	_____
Dining	_____	_____	_____
Private Dining	_____	_____	_____
Convenience Shop	_____	_____	_____
Woodworking	_____	_____	_____
Arts & Crafts	_____	_____	_____
Billiards	_____	_____	_____
Coffee Room	_____	_____	_____
Chapel	_____	_____	_____
Bank	_____	_____	_____
Post Office	_____	_____	_____
Barber/Beauty	_____	_____	_____
Health Assessment	_____	_____	_____
Multi-Purpose	_____	_____	_____
Lounge #1	_____	_____	_____
Lounge #2	_____	_____	_____
Lounge #3	_____	_____	_____
Lounge #4	_____	_____	_____
Library	_____	_____	_____
Security	_____	_____	_____
Exercise Room	_____	_____	_____
Sauna	_____	_____	_____
Whirlpool	_____	_____	_____
Greenhouse	_____	_____	_____
Solarium	_____	_____	_____

C. Site Requirements:

Room	Size (SF)	Finish Floor	Wall
Outdoor Patio	_____	_____	_____
Gazebo	_____	_____	_____
Raised Garden	_____	_____	_____
Walking/Jogging	_____	_____	_____
Passive Recreation	_____	_____	
Swimming Pool:	_____	Deck Area:	_____
Lake: Size:	_____	Depth:	_____
Guardhouse	_____	Key Card:	_____
Bus Stop	_____		
Shuffleboard	_____		
Horseshoes	_____		
Tennis Courts	_____		
Garages	_____ Number _____ Size _____		
Bathroom #2	_____	_____	_____
Exterior Storage	_____	_____	_____
Interior Storage	_____	_____	_____
Linen Closet	_____	_____	_____
Basement	_____	_____	_____
Balcony/Patio	_____	_____	_____
Solarium	_____	_____	_____
Porch	_____	_____	_____

D. Unit Design:

Unit Mix	No. Units	Per Unit	Required	Unit SF	S.F.
O BR	_____	_____	_____	_____	_____
1 BR	_____	_____	_____	_____	_____
1 BR/Den	_____	_____	_____	_____	_____
2 BR	_____	_____	_____	_____	_____
2 BR/Den	_____	_____	_____	_____	_____
TOTAL	_____	_____	_____	_____	_____

Patios/Balconies_____ Screened_____ Glassed_____
Laundry Hook-up_____
Basement_____
Solarium_____

Figure 5. Architectural Design Checklist
Retirement Housing (continued)

E. Utilities/Metering:

	Gas		Electric		Steam		Hot Water	
	Ind	Mas	Ind	Mas	Ind	Mas	Ind	Mas
1. Heat	___	___	___	___	___	___	___	___
2. Domestic Hot Water	___	___	___	___	___	___	___	___
3. Cooking	___	___	___	___	___	___	___	___
4. Air Condition.	___	___	___	___	___	___	___	___

F. Interior Details

1. Fireplace: Masonry_____ Metal_____ Stone_____

2. Trim:

	Size	Material	Type/Style	Finish
Baseboard	___	___	___	___
Casing	___	___	___	___
Doors-Interior	___	___	___	___
Doors-Exterior	___	___	___	___
Jambs	___	___	___	___
Handrails	___	___	___	___
Stairway	___	___	___	___
Stair Rail	___	___	___	___
Wainscoting	___	___	___	___
Crown Mold	___	___	___	___
Cabinets	___	___	___	___
Built-In Shelving	___	___	___	___
Paneling	___	___	___	___

1. Fireplace: Masonry_____ Metal_____ Stone_____

2. Trim:

	Size	Material	Type/Style	Finish
Closet Doors	___	___	___	___
Mail Box	___	___	___	___
Columns	___	___	___	___
Dividers	___	___	___	___
Medicine Cabinet	___	___	___	___
Closet Shelves	___	___	___	___

3. Type
   Lighting: Style_____   Finish_____

   Skylights_____

4. Windows: Type_____   Stools_____   Finish_____

   Grids_____   Screens_____   Storms_____

5. Appliances:

	0-BR	1-BR	2-BR
a. Size Range	___	___	___
b. Size Refrigerator	___	___	___
c. Range Hood	___	___	___
d. Dishwasher	___	___	___
e. Garbage Disposal	___	___	___
f. Trash Compactor	___	___	___

   g. Ranges - Number Burners_____   Self Clean_____
   h. Refrigerator: Self Defrost_____

6. Doors:
   a. Exterior Entry: Lock____ Deadbolt____ Chain Guard____
      Peepsite_____ Door Bell_____ Manual Knocker_____
      Lever_____ Knob_____ Finish_____
   b. Interior: Hardware_____ Bumper_____
      Lever_____ Knob_____ Finish_____
   c. Patio Door____ Sliding____ French____ Metal w/glass_____

7. Bathroom/Kitchen Fixtures:

	Type	Size	Finish	Material
Tub	___	___	_____	_____
Shower	___	___	_____	_____
Vanity	___	___	_____	_____
Commode	___	___	_____	_____
Medicine Cab.	___	___	_____	_____
Shower Rod	___	___	_____	_____

Figure 5. Architectural Design Checklist
Retirement Housing (continued)

Shower Rod   ____   ____   _____   _____
Laundry Tub   ____   ____   _____   _____
Jacuzzi   ____   ____   _____   _____
Faucets   ____   ____   _____   _____
Kitchen Sink   ____   ____   _____   _____
Backsplash   ____   ____   _____   _____
Countertop   ____   ____   _____   _____
Sprinkler   ____   ____   _____   _____

8. Interior Finisher:

	0-BR		1-BR		2-BR		3-BR		4-BR	
	FL	W	FL	W	FL	W	FL	W	FL	W
Living Room	__	__	__	__	__	__	__	__	__	__
Dining Room	__	__	__	__	__	__	__	__	__	__
Kitchen	__	__	__	__	__	__	__	__	__	__
Bath #1	__	__	__	__	__	__	__	__	__	__
Bath #2	__	__	__	__	__	__	__	__	__	__
MBR	__	__	__	__	__	__	__	__	__	__
BR #2	__	__	__	__	__	__	__	__	__	__
Den	__	__	__	__	__	__	__	__	__	__
Halls	__	__	__	__	__	__	__	__	__	__
Closets	__	__	__	__	__	__	__	__	__	__
Laundry	__	__	__	__	__	__	__	__	__	__
Basement	__	__	__	__	__	__	__	__	__	__

9. Electrical:
  a. Emergency: Call_____ Generator_____
  b. Elevators: Number_____ Size_____
  c. Fire Alarm: Auto_____ Manual Pull_____
  d. TV System: Antenna Per Unit____ Antenna/Building_____
   Master Antenna_____ Cable TV_____ Big Screen_____
   VCR_____ Closed Circuit_____
  e. Receptacle Heights:_____

10. Verify Furniture Arrangements:_____

11. Furnished/Unfurnished Units:_____

12. Verify Storage: Broom Closet_____ Linen Closet_____

Boiler_____ Wet_____ Dry_____
2-Pipe_____ 4-Pipe_____ Steam_____
Thru-Wall_____ Other_____ Type Equipment_____
Cool: F/A_____ Thru-Wall_____ 2-Pipe_____
4-Pipe_____ Other_____ Type Equipment_____

14. Mail Collection_____

7

The Facility Manager

by Peter Gerard

The facility manager is responsible for the most efficient and profitable use of his given resources, while considering the comfort, health, safety, and happiness of aging residents. A perpetual balance between accountability for the profit motive and sensitivity to the unique, varied, and changing needs of occupants must be achieved and maintained if a project is to succeed. Success also lies in meeting sponsor objectives. This means the provision the type and quality of service and product to the target market, such that the utilization or occupancy objectives are realized at an acceptable cost.

The following is a discussion of the special issues and considerations associated with the goal of the efficient and respon-

107

sible operation of congregate elderly housing. For the purposes
of this chapter it is assumed that decisions regarding location,
design, and construction have been made and target markets
and the nature and extent of services to be offered have been
identified.

Frequently, insufficient time and resources have been
committed to the analysis of the potential market for, and location and design of, facilities. This is particularly true of projects
built in recent years by inexperienced developers who were
merely responding to financial incentives. These factors are,
unfortunately, out of the hands of the person who must manage such a facility, and are therefore outside the scope of this
discussion.

Once a potential client becomes a resident, it is the facility
manager's responsibility to provide contracted services and to
maintain a high level of quality of product and service—re-
ferred to as "guest satisfaction" by those in the hotel industry.
It is in this area that some of the greatest changes in operational philosophy have occurred over the last few years. Once,
the elderly were warehoused in hospital-like settings as aging
was considered an illness. Today, this approach is unacceptable
in what has become a highly competitive, dynamic industry.
The emphasis is now on service as defined by the hospitality
industry, not the medical community.

The following is an outline of functional areas for facility
management.

Administration

The office of the Administrator or General Manager (GM)
should have overall responsibility for the facilities and operations—it is to him or her that all department heads report. In
the case where a third party management organization is used,
the GM reports to the director of operations or, in the case of

an owner/operator property, reports to the owner/sponsor. If a third party marketing/leasing organization is used, the GM also serves to coordinate operations with marketing activities.

The GM is responsible for the financial performance of the project, focusing on cost controls and labor management. He or she should be familiar with the project's financial statements, and must prepare monthly variance reports for senior management and owners.

Skill and sensitivity training are the GM's responsibility. The GM need not be directly involved with residential care, it should be the GM's responsibility to see that all staff are aware of the special needs and challenges associated with provision of services to the elderly. Constant training is critical to assure high service standards.

The GM's office should be directly responsible for and actively involved with all licensing and compliance matters. The GM should handle anything involving lawyers and litigation.

Accounting

While accounting and financial controls cannot assure the success of a project, the information they provide can significantly reduce the probability of failure and give on-site management the information they need to control operations. Accounting and financial information systems also provide owners and sponsors with data used to monitor the performance of managers and the overall project.

Our organization is committed to the concept of tight management, cash controls, and centralized accounting. We have found that it is significantly more efficient and cost effective to handle all accounting functions through a central processing group, for the following reasons:

- With centralized accounting, individual projects are relieved of significant payroll burdens and, more importantly, are freed from the constant challenge of attracting competent staff with a limited budget.

- The group attracts a high caliber staff because it spreads the higher payroll burden over a number of projects.

- A natural separation between operations and accounting is maintained, resulting in a significantly stronger control system.

- The costs of a centralized organization should be less than or equal to the direct labor cost of an on-site accounting staff.

- With centralized accounting you get higher quality output that is not dependent on a small group of people for the timely production of reports and information.

It is risky to depend on "rule of thumb" guidelines when establishing a cost structure for a particular project. Percentages will depend on unit and total revenue numbers, and totals will depend on the nature and efficiency of the particular facility, and the phase of "lease-up" that the project is in. Like a hotel, and unlike other types of commercial and multi-family real estate, a significant percentage of services must be maintained regardless of occupancy levels.

Tenant Services

The success of an organization is dependent on its ability to deliver what its customers want. Therefore, it is essential that an organization is constantly aware of its customer's desires. The tenant services department is responsible for the establishment of communication channels with residents and for the provision of activities planning, transportation, and other ancillary services. This contact between residents and tenant services is the primary information channel for management to monitor its performance, so it is critical that interaction with residents be regular and routine to ensure the quality and timeliness of feedback.

Tenant services is headed by the activities director whose primary responsibility is to provide for the non-lodging and food needs of the residents. This person and all department staff must be sensitive to the makeup of the resident population, particularly their physical limitations.

Marketing

During the "lease-up" phase of a project, marketing is usually handled by a separate, specialized marketing organization. During this period, the primary function of the facility management staff is to provide support for this group and coordinate schedules and activities to assist in marketing. At the completion of this initial phase, however, the facility manager and marketing department usually assume the marketing function. This department is responsible for vacancy projection and the maintenance of communication channels through the use of advertising and direct mail. Open houses or tenant parties where residents may invite non-tenant friends also produce qualified leads.

From a marketing perspective, it is critical that one understand that a move to a retirement home is perceived by potential residents as a monumental change in lifestyle. Patience, empathy, and perseverance are essential components of a successful, ongoing marketing program.

Housekeeping

A strong housekeeping department is essential to the success of any project. The cleanliness and general condition of the public space has a major influence on resident satisfaction. We recommend that a weekly housecleaning service be a requirement for all units, with more frequent service an option. This provides a way for the operator to ensure adequate facility maintenance while monitoring the condition of residents.

The housekeeping staff should be trained to recognize signs of physical or mental distress. Because they are in constant contact with tenants and their personal living quarters, housekeeping staff must be particularly sensitive to the privacy and dignity of residents.

Food Service

The food service department is the most important operating department for resident satisfaction, as well as one of the most difficult to manage from a cost standpoint. Most projects offer regular meal service and most contracts provide for one meal per day (usually dinner), with breakfast and lunch optional. The quality and attractiveness of the food and setting is very important.

Meal time is a time for the residents to gather, visit, and interact. If things are going well, this can be a very positive assembly. If residents are dissatisfied, however, the dining room is where the level of dissatisfaction will escalate. Therefore, it is crucial that food service personnel be sensitive to the needs and comments of the residents. We suggest that tenant service staff make it a point to have staff members at all meals, always.

Staffing, menu composition, and portion size are the main cost control factors in food service. Resident profiles are an important source of information for the establishment of guide-lines for these variables.

Maintenance

The maintenance department is not only responsible for keep-ing the assets productive, it can also improve and maintain a positive resident attitude toward the project. Timely and sensi-tive responses to tenant requests can do much to strengthen the management/resident relationship. Like the housekeeping de-partment, this group has frequent tenant contact—they can serve to monitor residents and alert staff of potential problems.

Security

Security is one of the gravest concerns of the elderly. It is im-portant that a project provide tangible evidence of security to the residents. In addition to in room monitoring and alert sys-tems, persons clearly identified as security personnel must be present at all times. As with all departments, security staff must be sensitive to the particular needs and concerns of resi-dents.

Health Care

The nature and extent health care services provided is, to a large extent, determined by the project physical plant and the original positioning of the facility in the market. Some degree of health care service is necessary in all types of projects.

It is essential that all projects address this need either with on-site facilities or a formal relationship with third party pro-viders.

Conclusion

The operation of an elderly housing facility today is very different from what it once was. High levels of service and hospitality are critical to project success in today's marketplace. A growing target population and changing demographics spell opportunity for the cagey investor, but retirement projects must be managed with an open, understanding, and compassionate attitude. Sensitivity to the special needs and of elderly residents is essential for the well being of tenants, and of the bottom line.

8

Pitfalls in the Senior Housing Industry

by Richard R. Jaffe

With advanced medical techniques and better health care and nutrition, the United States has experienced a population increase in the 65-year plus age bracket, with a dramatic rise in the 80-to 85-year bracket. This growth in the elderly population should result in windfalls for the retirement housing industry; unfortunately, that business has seen many workouts and foreclosures in recent years.

Churches and fraternal organizations first recognized this demographic trend and identified a need to provide seniors with housing. In the late 1970s, these not-for-profit organizations successfully focused on a "lifecare concept" and system of endowment investment programs to provide continuous care for the rest of senior tenants' lives. A slumping market for residential apartments, shopping centers, and small office buildings found developers turning to rental retirement housing as a sub-industry with great potential returns.

In the early '80s, financial institutions aggressively sought to place funds into real estate development. This availability of investment dollars, large number of developers, and concentrated building in only a few geographic areas resulted in early market saturation, followed by a glut of non-performing or troubled retirement housing communities. The number of firms specializing in rehabilitating these troubled assets increased as developers sought corrective action to prevent foreclosure.

The following are key factors that have put many facilities into bankruptcy.

Poor Location

Developers of retirement communities frequently overlook the impact that location has on their prospective tenants' lifestyles. The facility must be close to banks, public transportation, shopping centers, restaurants, a post office, and most importantly, to hospital or physician services. A high crime rate or isolated location will spell failure for the project, as will a low population of seniors in the area.

Saturated Market

Even a well-operated and attractive facility may fail in a market which has an oversupply of similar facilities. A highly-competitive, saturated marketplace will squeeze out excess units.

Poor Facility Planning/Unattractive Design

If a retirement community is markedly different from the local character and tastes of the surrounding community, local senior residents will be reluctant to leave their present homes. For example, building a high-rise facility in an essentially low-rise community would exemplify poor facility planning.

Market Area Pricing

Facility and service fees must be commensurate with the potential resident group's ability to pay.

Overpriced Services

The cost for a service amenities package, bundled or unbundled, is a component of the residents' total living cost. Seniors' spending habits are often conservative—they know a good value, and also when services and benefits do not warrant the asking price.

Insufficient Marketing

Substantial capital should be available for advertising and promotion, both initial and ongoing. Unrealistically high move-in projections can result in serious underestimation of the marketing effort and expenses needed to achieve full occupancy.

Poor Lead Generation

An adequate advertising and promotion program is critical to fill a new retirement community. Sufficient community visibility is required to stimulate strong market interest and to create inquiry and visitation traffic, all of which produce sales. On-site visits and contacts are required to create and close sales in the senior housing industry. (An unsuccessful advertising campaign should be reviewed to ensure the intended message is being communicated, and that the ads are reaching the target audience. These factors are, of course, limited by the ad budget.) Are the ads, marketing and promotion concentrated on a small geographical area? Are ads misleading to customers or generating unqualified prospect leads? Are visiting potentials too young, financially unqualified, or too frail to live independently?

Poor Sales Team

Sales staff may lack skills, incentives, knowledge of proven techniques, or selling tools such as literature, maps, models, or visual aids. Examine the qualifications of the Marketing Director, his compensation package, selling skills, and time management. "Not ready yet" is the most often presented and most difficult to overcome customer objection. Retirement living must be presented as a positive change in lifestyle. Follow-up is critical. Four to seven visits are required to convert a qualified prospect to a resident. An adequate tracking system is essential to capture these potential customers.

Lack Of Adequate Operating Capital

Business plan budgets must be conservative. Operating costs should be overestimated to allow for unexpected expenses and overruns. Inadequate cash flow to cover these losses could force a project into bankruptcy before achieving its break even point.

Poor Management

The degree of risk to a project's success is proportional to the competence and experience of its management. Management must be able to limit costs to budgeted amounts, maintain high levels of employee performance, be insightful and sensitive in dealing with senior citizens, and monitor the financial needs of the facility. Goodwill, maintained between management and the retirement community, will promote the facility through "word of mouth," increasing move-ins.

Low Occupancy

Inadequate move-in rates or a high cancellation rate of prior commitments will result in low occupancy. Low move-in rates are usually the result of poor advertising, a substandard referral or networking system, a negative project reputation, or an insufficient pool of local residents who are qualified in age and income.

Reasons for a negative reputation should be examined and corrected. What is important to the residents? Adequate facility maintenance and food services are very important to seniors. Negative word of mouth travels quickly in a tight-knit senior community and will keep away potential tenants.

Contact with local church groups, business community leaders, health-care professionals, and neighborhood associations can strengthen a referral or networking system. Retirement facility tenants usually have very close ties within the community and in the immediate vicinity, having been residents there themselves.

A low senior population or stiff competition among comparable retirement projects can result in slow move-ins, as can a soft real estate market because prospective tenants may have difficulty selling their current homes.

Poor Fiscal Management

Failure to collect timely rents and excessive free-rent or low-rent specials can disrupt cash flow. Internal controls such as audit trails, control of cash disbursements, and similar checks and balances must be in place to deter fraud, theft, and embezzlement.

High Operating Costs

Staffing levels at or under those detailed in the business plan are more desirable than instituting layoffs that result from overstaffing. A staffing chart with job descriptions for personnel positions is necessary for monitoring personnel costs.

Bundled services may have to be dismantled, keeping only the most frequently used services as part of the package. Expensive or seldom used services may be offered "a la carte". Purchasing procedures should be examined—excess costs can be lowered by simple comparison shopping and common-sense waste minimization.

High Debt Levels

Excessive debt load usually results at the inception of a project. Over-leveraged financing coupled with high interest rates can cause debt levels which are too high to be serviced from the property cashflow. Excessive up-front developer fees and points can bleed away capital badly needed for operations, at a time the project needs to build and maintain reserves. Amenities should be consistent with projected rental or service fees that the particular market can afford for the project.

Low Rents

Poor pre-marketing may precipitate the need to lease-up quickly, resulting in many leases being signed at unrealistically low rents relative to the market. The project will then lack sufficient daily revenues to cover the cost of providing promised, contracted services. Rent increases should be justified to the resident community and presented only as one alternative to correct insufficient operating revenues.

High Cancellation Rates

Conceptual changes during facility construction can increase cancellations, and an overly long construction period can create a perception of financial instability. The sales and marketing team must follow-up and maintain frequent contact with a potential resident after he or she makes a deposit. The prospect may be lured away by a competitor or influenced by children or heirs. Honesty and accuracy by the sales team is critical to maintain client trust and prevent the "buyer remorse" that may result in cancellation. Deteriorating health may require a potential move-in to seek a different facility with a higher level of care; evaluate the prospect's health status before including them in your reserved unit backlog. Unforseen financial crises can affect a prospect's ability to pay.

Understanding the reasons for failure detailed here may save untold frustration and financial difficulty. The senior housing industry offers unlimited potential for those developers, investors, and managers that take the time to learn from other's mistakes. The most costly way to solve a retirement community problem is by trial and error; the cost of this approach will always far exceed the cost of utilizing management consulting teams with industry-specific experience to revitalize troubled facilities.

9

The Anatomy
of a Workout

by Richard R. Jaffe

In the first frantic moments of a workout, a crisis atmosphere prevails. I sometimes compare this situation to what occurs in a hospital emergency room. The doctor (project workout specialist) has to work quickly to stop the bleeding and stabilize the patient's vital signs. It is only when the patient's condition is on more sure footing that he can be moved to where planned care may begin in a calmer atmosphere. But those first steps are critical to saving a project in the same way that they are to an emergency room patient.

This chapter will outline the steps that I consider to be essential in working out a troubled retirement community or

123

senior care facility. As you will see, this discussion is not a legal primer but rather offers some thoughts for project managers to consider in the workout of their senior housing problems. As always, legal counsel should be retained to advise and protect the owner's or developer's interest in a project.

A troubled project is never a complete surprise. Tenants, staff, and the community at large usually become aware that some services are slipping. The owner or developer may have missed several mortgage payments, so the lender is also aware that trouble is on the horizon and is probably already weighing its options.

The crisis is brought on when some unexpected event jeopardizes the position and interest of the property owner or developer. The posting for foreclosure by one of the lenders is just such an event. Another is when creditors appear on site to repossess equipment or fixtures because payments are late or management has failed to communicate with the lender.

The following are steps that should be taken immediately to help stem the crisis.

Stabilize the attitude of existing residents. Honesty and an open flow of communication with tenants is critical. They must be provided a complete and honest assessment of current problems. You must retain as many paying residents as possible during a workout. Their confidence and trust must be preserved.

Obtain working capital. The facility will be placed on COD terms by suppliers during the workout, so the development of a financial plan that will obtain new working capital for daily operations is important. Working capital will come from either new investors or from those who have already lent your business significant sums of money. They hope that your plan will enable them to be repaid and will often provide only a limited amount of advances.

Motivate and retain your employees. The greatest asset that your property can have is loyal, competent employees. Discuss with them your game plan, the proposed solution, and their role on your team. Their natural tendency will be to "cut and run." These people are the group to whom your residents look for support. It will be difficult to build confidence with your residents if you cannot do so with your own employees. Deliveries of items necessary for continued daily operations will arrive late, incomplete, or not at all. Resolving these matters will waste much of your time and concentration, and may frustrate you—be sure not to worry your employees or residents with any public display of irritation.

The early weeks of a workout are the most difficult, busiest, and the most important. You will probably not realize that your local town has so many lawyers. You will hear from them all in the first few weeks, each one representing a creditor who wants to be paid. You will be inundated with paper, phone calls, letters on behalf of creditors, and from the creditors themselves. They want to know how you plan to handle this matter and how they can qualify as secured or priority creditors. How you handle your initial dealings with their lawyers will influence how difficult the next few weeks will be for you. If you deal with them with candidly and they believe your good intentions, competency, and therefore feel there exists a chance for a successful workout of this problem, they will focus their attention on other creditor cases they consider more urgent. The more time they spend on their other matters, the more time you will have to get your plan of reorganization underway.

The most important early meeting will be with your largest creditors, including your mortgage holder, who most wants to see these problems resolved. Remember that the mortgage lender has access to large capital resources and is therefore an excellent potential source of continued financing. Be prepared for expensive and difficult negotiations to restructure your obligations. Plan on either a diminished equity or a loss of equity entirely. The value of your project versus debt and equity invested will greatly influence your ability to refinance the first mortgage, secure a second mortgage, or find alternate financing to furnish new capital.

Workouts begin before foreclosure and may be handled either in or out of court. The sooner that management contacts creditors and develops an open dialogue of disclosure, the better the chance that the out of court route can be used. The immediate goal is to keep creditors from taking precipitous or premature legal action on their loans or debts. Out of court workouts avoid costly legal fees and court costs.

If the matter must be handled through the judicial system, there are two alternatives—Chapter 11 (voluntary) or Chapter 7 (involuntary) bankruptcy proceedings. Chapter 11 is the better route because it permits a substantial rehabilitation of the creditors.

Unfortunately, Chapter 11 bankruptcy proceedings succeed in rehabilitating the creditor only about 20 to 25 percent of the time. (By contrast, workouts performed out of court succeed in about 65 to 75 percent of cases.) In the crisis mode, a project's creditors become instant adversaries. Each party will vie to position themselves for the highest priority on the payment schedule.

The filing of a Chapter 11 petition does not cancel debts, but places a temporary stay on payments until debts are cataloged, prioritized, and filed with the courts. Then the development of a reorganization plan begins. This plan requires the approval of the majority of the creditors and the court. One of the problems with the filing of a Chapter 11 petition is that it is virtually impossible for a facility to continue to function without a new source of cash or credit.

Close monitoring of cash flow will be critical in the ensuing weeks because in a workout "Cash is king." Maximization of cash flow will give you the ability to operate during the workout period. You must continue to provide promised services to residents. Deciding which nonessentials to eliminate will be one of your toughest decisions—retain only those things necessary to keep your project alive and competitive in the market. It is certain that you will have to defer some noncritical maintenance that will not affect day-to-day operations or the ability to retain residents and gain new ones.

Timeliness and quick action is essential during this period. Seek advice from experienced professionals who can give you immediate answers without the costs and delays of trial and error. The services of an attorney who is familiar with bankruptcy matters and is familiar with retirement housing or healthcare-related properties should be part of this team of experts.

The advice of a consultant experienced with workouts is also invaluable, and will save you considerable money in the long run. The consultant provides "damage control" and can make the tough decisions that significantly increase cash flow and can, most of all, *anticipate* the problems that may arise. Objective in decision making, a consultant can address issues and problems on the strength of his or her experience. This will be a learning experience for you and should enable you to prevent these problems from recurring in this project and future projects.

Accounting expertise is also crucial because you will need accounting reports to be produced quickly and accurately. Clear, accurate financials are essential to gain the confidence of creditors and lenders. They must be provided an unclouded financial picture of your project and your plan for a successful turnaround. A new face managing your financials will be more credible to creditors if you and/or your previous accountant have made unkept promises.

National trade associations are a good source of names of consultants, advisers, and lawyers familiar with both workouts and retirement housing. Retirement housing and healthcare industry trade publications and journals usually contain advertisements of member firms that proffer these services.

In conclusion, I feel there are four essential principles to follow in the workout of troubled properties:

Understand your project thoroughly. You must be able to define problems objectively. Chances are, you probably need an experienced outside consultant and who can address problems in a fresh, detached manner.

Focus on your present resources. Analyze your project to identify strengths, weaknesses and unencumbered assets—those positive ingredients on which you may base the project's turnaround. You may have to go back to the negotiating table and assume additional financial risks to obtain guarantees for the injection of new capital and resources to resolve the project's present financial problems.

Maintain a continuous dialogue with creditors. Provide complete, frequent, and accurate communications and financials between involved parties. Identify problems and initiate intelligent and quick solutions.

Deal fairly with everyone involved in the project. A calm, equitable, and cooperative working environment is the most efficient way to resolve differences. Energy spent vying for strategic position must be minimized so creditors will understand the relation of teamwork to the ultimate recovery of their investment.

It is impossible to cover everything that occurs in a workout in one chapter of a book. The ideas presented here are accumulated from experience and may help management focus on those things necessary to put a troubled project on the road to recovery. Managers should always remember that the most costly way to salvage a retirement community problem is by the trial and error method. Expensive mistakes will always exceed fees paid to an interim expert.

Publications
and Associations

Publications

Medical Economics
Contemporary Long-Term Care
Journal of Housing for the Elderly
Multi-Housing News
Topics in Health Care Financing
Modern Healthcare
Healthcare Financial Management
Retirement Housing Report
Real Estate Issues
Housing the Elderly
Journal of Property Management
Journal of Long Term Home Health Care

Journal of Independent Living
Senior Housing News
Generations
American Health Care Association Journal
Mature Market Report
50 Plus

Associations

American Association of Homes for the Aging (AAHA)
1050 17th St., N.W.
Washington, D.C. 20036
(202) 296-5960

American Association of Retired People (AARP)
1909 K St., N.W.
Washington, D.C. 20049
(202) 872-4700

National Association of Independent Living Centers
1501 Lee Highway, Suite 205
Arlington, VA 22209
(703) 872-1717

National Association of Senior Living Industries
125 Cathedral St.
Annapolis, MD 21401
(301) 263-0991

National Council on Aging
600 Maryland Ave., S.W.
Washington, D.C.
(202) 479-1200

Glossary

A

AAA tenant: A prime tenant who has the highest credit rating.

absentee ownership: Ownership of property (usually income producing) by a non-occupant who employs others to manage and maintain the property.

absorption: The level of property units rented or sold after which price concessions must be made for market demand to continue at current levels. Used to determine the feasibility of new residential or commercial construction.

acceptance letter: A document signed by a construction loan borrower stating that all work is complete and of acceptable quality.

accommodation party: A person who lends his name to guarantee a loan for another by signing a note, bill, or other negotiable instrument; the endorser becomes the guarantor of the loan and is therefore responsible for its repayment.

acquisition cost: In a HUD/FHA transaction, the price the borrower paid for the property plus any of the following costs: closing, repairs, or financing (except discounts in other than a refinance transaction). Does not include prepaid discounts in a purchase transaction, mortgage insurance premiums, or similar add-ons.

adaptive re-use: The rehabilitation of old property for a new purpose.

allowance for vacancy and income loss: In accounting, an estimated amount reflecting probable vacancy, non-payment of rent by tenants, and any other income loss. These funds are set aside to cover either expected or unanticipated income losses.

amenity: A feature that enhances property value. Examples are off-street reserved parking within a condominium community, the proximity of public transportation, tennis courts, or a swimming pool.

amount to make the project operational (AMPO): An allowance, ordinarily a percentage of the replacement cost, that can be included in the mortgage insured by HUD/FHA to provide a nonprofit sponsor with working capital during the initial period of operation of a project.

apartment: A complete and separate living unit in a building containing at least one other like unit.

B

bond: An interest-bearing certificate of debt of a government or a business corporation. In real estate, a bond is a written obligation usually secured by a mortgage or a trust deed.

break-even point: The figure at which occupancy income is equal to all required expenses and debt service. Used to determine the amount of cash flow necessary to operate a residential or commercial property.

builder-seller sponsor: A project sponsor specifically organized to build or rehabilitate and sell a project immediately upon completion to a private, nonprofit organization, at the certified cost of the project. The nonprofit sponsor buys a total package.

builder's and sponsor's profit and risk allowance (BSPRA): A credit against the required equity contribution in HUD/FHA insurance programs granted the developer for its services in sponsoring and building the project.

C

certificate of completion: A document issued by an architect or engineer stating that construction is completed in accordance with the terms, conditions, approved plans, and specifications.

certificate of occupancy: Written authorization given by a local municipality that allows a newly completed or substantially renovated structure to be inhabited.

common area: An area owned by the owners or tenants of a complex or subdivision, for the common use of residents.

community apartment project: Multiple ownership of an apartment in which each owner is a tenant-in-common.

condominium: A form of property ownership whereby the purchaser receives title to the unit and a proportionate interest in common areas.

congregate housing: A specially designed apartment complex that provides shelter, meals, housekeeping, transportation, and social activities.

construction costs: All costs incurred in the completion of a construction project, including land, labor, overhead, and builder's profit.

construction loan: A short-term, interim loan for financing the cost of construction. The lender advances funds to the builder at periodic intervals as work progresses.

conventional financing: In real estate, mortgage financing which is not insured or guaranteed by a government agency such as HUD/FHA, VA, or the Farmers Home Administration.

cooperative: In real estate, a form of multiple ownership in which a corporation or business trust entity holds title to a property, (usually an apartment complex) and grants occupancy rights to shareholder tenants through proprietary leases. Also called a co-op.

corporation: A business entity owned by a group of owners, called stockholders. A corporation is considered an artificial person under law.

D

debt capital: Money loaned at an agreed interest rate for a fixed term of years; distinguished from equity capital which is money invested by owners (shareholders) for use in business operations.

debt service: A borrower's periodic mortgage payments comprised of principal plus interest on the unpaid mortgage balance.

developer: A person or entity who prepares raw land for building sites or rehabilitates existing buildings.

development process: The process through which development projects are conceived, initiated, analyzed, financed, designed, built, and managed.

direct costs: Labor and materials costs of construction, excluding overhead.

dwelling unit: Living quarters occupied, or intended for occupancy, by a household.

E

equity capital: Money invested by shareholders who are owners and who receive a share of profits.

equity participation: The right of a lender to a share in the gross profits, net profits, or net proceeds in the event of sale or refinance of a property on which the lender has made a loan. Also known as an "equity kicker."

F

fair market rent: An amount determined by HUD to be the cost of modest, non-luxury rental units in a specific market area.

feasibility study: A detailed investigation and analysis conducted to determine the financial, economic, technical, or other advisability of a proposed project.

Federal Housing Administration (FHA): A federal agency within the Department of Housing and Urban Development (HUD) that provides mortgage insurance for residential mortgages and sets standards for construction and underwriting. The FHA does not lend money, nor does it plan or construct housing.

FHA loan: A loan made through an approved lender and insured by the Federal Housing Administration. While there are limits to the size of FHA loans, they are intended to finance moderately priced homes.

FHA value: The value established by the FHA as the basis for determining the maximum mortgage amount that may be insured on a specific property. The FHA value is the sum of the appraised value of the property plus HUD/FHA's estimate of closing costs.

financing package: The financing vehicles used to fund a project, including mortgages, partnerships, joint venture capital interest, stock ownership, or any financial arrangement.

G

general partner: The co-owner of a real estate venture who is liable for all debts and other obligations of the venture as well as for the management and operation of the partnership. The general partner controls the business and can take actions that are binding on the other partners.

H

HUD: The Department of Housing and Urban Development. A governmental entity responsible for the implementation and administration of housing and urban development programs. HUD was established by the Housing and Urban Development Act of 1965 to supersede the Housing and Home Finance Agency.

hybrid investment: An investment that is a mix of debt and equity.

I

income participation: A loan arrangement wherein the lender shares in property income as well as interest earned on the loan.

income property: Real estate developed or improved to produce income.

institutional lender: A financial institution that lends to the public. Examples are mutual savings banks, life insurance companies, commercial banks, pension and trust funds, and savings and loan associations.

interest rate swap: A transaction in which two parties trade individual financing advantages to produce more favorable borrowing terms for each party. Normally, one party will wish a fixed interest rate and the other a variable rate.

investor sponsor: In cooperative housing programs, a private, profit-making organization that undertakes the development of housing projects for sale at a profit to non-profit cooperative corporations.

J

joint venture: An association formed for a specific purpose and duration between two or more parties to own and/or develop real estate. A joint venture may take a variety of legal forms including partnership, tenancy in common, or corporation.

K

kicker: Term describing any benefit to a lender above ordinary fixed-interest payments. It may be an equity position in a property or a percentage participation in the income stream.

L

life care communities: Elaborately designed complexes structured to address the problems of both shelter and health care. In this type of facility, meals, housekeeping, and medical care are available for a fee.

limited partnership: A form of business ownership that consists of one or more general partners who are fully liable, and one or more limited partners who are liable only for the amount of their investment.

line of credit: An agreement by a commercial bank or other financial institution to extend credit up to a certain amount for a certain time to a specific borrower.

loan-to-value ratio: The ratio of mortgage amount to appraised value or sales price of real property. Used by lenders to determine maximum loan amounts as set by law.

M

market rent: The price a tenant pays a landlord for the use and occupancy of real property based on current prices for comparable property.

market study: The projection of demand for a specific type of property or project, obtained by analyzing data on sales volume, rents, vacancies, turnover, consumer preferences, and real estate prices in the surrounding area for similar properties.

multifamily development: A complex consisting of two or more residential buildings as a part of a single development. Generally associated with garden apartments, townhouses, and highrise apartment complexes.

multifamily housing: A building with more than four residential units.

multifamily mortgage: A mortgage on a dwelling that is designed to house more than four families, such as a highrise apartment complex.

mutual savings banks: An institution owned by its depositors as evidenced by certificates of deposit rather than stock. These institutions are active in long-term real estate financing, as opposed to commercial banks which concentrate on short-term loans.

N

net rentable area: The actual square footage of a building that can be rented. Halls, lobbies, stairways, elevator shafts, maintenance areas, and other common areas may or may not be included, depending on the custom of the locality.

not-for-profit sponsor: A group not motivated by profit that backs a housing project. Units can be rented on a nonprofit basis or the sponsor can allow individual, cooperative, or condominium ownership.

P

participation loan: A financing arrangement in which a mortgage lender receives a portion of cash flow, gross revenue, or shares of ownership of a real estate venture as a part of the loan. Also called a kicker.

partnership: A business association of two or more owners who share in the profits and losses of the business. Partners are jointly and severally liable for the debts of the enterprise.

passive investor: An investor who has no active role in the operation or construction of a business or project, and who participates only to earn a return on and of his investment.

point: An amount equal to one percent of the principal amount of an investment or note. Loan discount points are a one-time charge assessed at closing by the lender to increase the yield on the mortgage loan to a competitive position with other types of investments.

pro forma statement: A financial or accounting statement using estimates and assumptions to project income and the performance of real property over a period of time.

project costs: Total cost of the project including professional compensation, land costs, furnishings and equipment, financing, construction costs, and other charges.

R

rent-up period: The period after construction that a rental property requires to achieve projected stabilized income and occupancy levels.

retirement community: A planned community for those of retirement age, providing attractively sized and priced dwelling units, and offering construction features, amenities and locations for aging residents.

S

savings and loan association: A mutual or stock association chartered and regulated by the Office of Thrift Supervision. Traditionally, deposits are invested in residential mortgage loans, although savings and loans now have broader lending powers.

seed money: Funds required to start a development project, generally advanced by a developer or equity owner as a capital contribution to the project. Also called front-end money or front money.

T

tenant: One who is not the owner but occupies real property under consent of the owner and in subordination to the owner's title. The tenant is entitled to exclusive possession, use, and enjoyment of the property, usually for a time and amount specified in the lease.

V

vacancy factor: The percentage of gross rental income that represents vacant units.

vacancy rate: The ratio between the number of vacant units and the total number of units in a multi-tenant building or development.

venture capital: Capital put in highly risky or speculative investments.

Index

A

B